PRAISE FOR *KNOW WHAT YOU DON'T KNOW*

"Higher education doesn't suffer from a lack of effort, it suffers from a lack of informed courage. Bart Caylor's *Know What You Don't Know* is a call to leaders to stop outsourcing judgment and start leading with curiosity, discipline, and moral clarity. I've had the privilege of working alongside Bart in consulting environments and as a client institution president, and what separates him is his insistence on accountability—to data, to students, and to mission. This book doesn't coddle leaders. It equips them. And that's exactly what this moment in higher education demands."

—JAMIE CARIDI, Interim President, Bethany College (West Virginia) / Terra Firma Consulting

"Bart Caylor's *Know What You Don't Know* is an insightful and practical guide for higher education leaders seeking long-term, data-driven sustainability. Caylor offers clear strategies and thoughtful tools to help institutions ask the right questions of their marketing efforts and stand out authentically—becoming the "zebra in a herd of horses." His emphasis on developing the right framework and recognizing AI as an intelligent, collaborative partner reflects a rapidly evolving landscape that leaders must be prepared to navigate. I value the book's honesty, clarity, and actionable direction."

—AMY BRAGG CAREY, President, Friends University

"As president of the Council for Christian Colleges & Universities, I highly recommend this book. Caylor's guidance empowers leaders to move beyond survival, fostering sustainable growth and distinctiveness. His wisdom and practical advice are essential for anyone committed to advancing Christian higher education.

Bart Caylor's *Know What You Don't Know* is an indispensable guide for presidents and senior marketing leaders in higher education. Caylor pinpoints the real challenge: a lack of marketing literacy at the top, which can lead to costly missteps and missed opportunities. He doesn't ask leaders to become technical experts, but to develop practical wisdom and discernment. This enables them to pose effective questions, assess strategies accurately, and ensure marketing supports the institution's mission.

The book's actionable frameworks, including the Four P's, and its emphasis on authentic storytelling, generational diversity, and AI, are especially relevant for today's rapidly changing landscape. Caylor's insights help leaders avoid common pitfalls, such as confusing advertising with true marketing or relying on vanity campaigns."

—DAVID HOAG, President, CCCU

"In a recent informal study, we discovered that the institutions enjoying enrollment success had stable leadership at the presidential and senior enrollment management levels. But there's a catch: While stability helped, the effective leaders weren't using static tools and approaches. That's where a book like the one in your hands is invaluable. Bart mines a cornucopia of practical wisdom to help presidents give innovative leadership to arguably one of the most crucial disciplines today—finding, attracting, and enrolling students. Bart's cutting-edge experience, and years of trust-building with presidents, make him an ideal guide in today's changing and demanding environment."

—DAVID WRIGHT, Former President, Indiana Wesleyaan University

"Bart Caylor has winsomely assessed the current marketing challenges and opportunities for higher education, including the use and influence of Artificial Intelligence. The complexity and rapid pace of change faced by today's higher education leaders make managing institutional influence difficult and unwieldy. The pressure for results and the highly polarized culture are significant obstacles for those who wish to stabilize or advance the campuses we serve; however, Bart offers simple, grounded tools leaders can use to understand marketing and creatively address the rapidly changing environment. Each chapter (2 through 13) offers today's higher education leader an opportunity to "Take Action." In these sections, Bart offers leader-learners the chance to reflect and to help identify the questions we should be asking the marketing teams on our campuses. This is an important and insightful read for any leader looking to address the marketing needs of today's higher education landscape."

—DR. BRAD JOHNSON, President, College of the Ozarks

Know What You Don't Know is ultimately a book about leadership—leadership in a moment when higher education faces pressures unlike anything in recent memory. Bart Caylor names these challenges with clarity and courage: the enrollment cliff that has arrived, the search cliff that is accelerating, the dramatic shifts in generational expectations, and the pervasive fragmentation of data systems that leaves institutions "data rich but insight poor." He also addresses one of the most misunderstood forces shaping the sector—AI—and reframes it not as a threat or shortcut, but as a new form of "institutional electricity," capable of accelerating human judgment and improving the quality of leadership decisions. Caylor's central message is both humbling and empowering: leaders don't need to be marketing experts, but they do need enough literacy to ask better questions, challenge assumptions, and guide strategy with confidence. If leaders want to make the level of impact that is genuinely expected of them today, this literacy is no longer optional—it is foundational. Through practical frameworks, clear explanations, and a consistently student-centered lens, Caylor shows leaders how to "work the problem" with the same resourcefulness and composure that saved Apollo 13. This book is timely, insightful, and essential for anyone committed to leading with wisdom and courage."

—KIKO SUAREZ, C-Suite Advisor, Leadership Development,
   Keynote Speaker Higher Education, Nonprofit and
   Philanthropic Sectors

"Bart Caylor is truly one of the visionaries in our space. *Know What You Don't Know* is a masterful distillation of the insights leaders are urgently seeking as they navigate marketing, enrollment strategy, and the rapidly shifting landscape we all share. As an edtech leader building tools to support student engagement and recruitment, I face many of the same pressures as campus leaders: changing student behavior, the rise of AI, the need for smarter marketing investment, and the challenge of aligning teams around clear, data-driven strategy. Bart speaks directly to those realities. What sets Bart apart is his ability to translate complex concepts such as AI adoption, digital media strategy, brand positioning, and program viability into practical guidance leaders can use immediately. His call for courageous, student-centered, data-informed leadership resonates across the entire higher ed ecosystem, from enrollment offices to the companies that serve them. Bart's work has always pushed our industry forward, but this book feels especially essential. *Know What You Don't Know* is not just timely; it is transformative. Every enrollment leader, and every leader supporting higher education, should read it."

—VANESSA DIDYK, CEO, ZeeMee

"We live in a day when the way things have been done will no longer work. Colleges face a shrinking pool of applicants, and the only way to keep going is to increase market share. Bart Caylor provides a needed primer on marketing, designed to change the way institutions view the people they desire to serve. Read this and then deploy his time-tested wisdom. It could be the difference between a sustainable path forward and a wind-down."

—JEFF SPEAR, Former President, CFO Colleague

"Leaders in higher education should always take note of what Bart Caylor is thinking. Caylor has spent the bulk of his long and successful professional career seeking to understand the ever-evolving world of marketing to young adults (and their well-intentioned, but often under-informed, parents), who together are considering attendance at an institution of higher education.

Caylor is well aware of the oddities and naiveties that are evidenced in that decision-making process. He also has observed, first hand, the sea change in the art and science of marketing that has occurred since the 1980s. Moreover, he has worked closely with countless college and university leaders (at every level), both public and private, who are desperately looking to marketing as a potential savior of lackluster academic programs, mission drift, declining enrollments, questionable reputations, needy campus facilities, and deepening financial stress.

Here we have a prime example of the value Caylor brings to the table. With his easily accessible writing style, and thirteen short chapters, Caylor weaves into his writing a fascinating look at: (1) the history of marketing to higher education; (2) how that art/science has evolved and professionalized over the last four decades; and (3) where it stands currently. Caylor then provides the reader with a tutorial on the realities of today's complex and, at times, confusing world of marketing. He defines and explains current terms of art and describes marketing processes, procedures, and rationales. Caylor provides the reader-leader with a practical understanding of marketing upon which to engage and move forward.

More importantly, Caylor speaks directly to college and university leaders and the role they must play to engage and to surmount the marketing challenges that confront higher education. Recognizing that the engine does not run without fuel, he emphasizes the critical need for decisive presidential and board leadership in creating a successful marketing program. These are, after all, existential issues. Caylor notes that successful institutional marketing is "mission-critical," and not something to be treated casually or set aside for another day. He cautions his readers, however, that the attitude one approaches the marketing task is of the greatest importance if one desires to truly have institutional impact and success. Institutional leaders should approach the task of institutional marketing not as experts or know-it-alls, but rather as humble students of a rapidly-evolving and mission-critical art and science upon which their futures, and their institution's survival, are staked. As an initial step, and to be truly successful, they should seek first to "know what they don't know"... which is a lot. It is worth sitting at Caylor's feet. When he speaks, higher education should listen."

—PAUL LOWELL HAINES, Former President, Taylor University

"I have known Bart Caylor for years, and one thing has always been true. When Bart talks, leaders listen. They usually take notes and sometimes rethink their entire strategy. *Know What You Don't Know* is Bart at his best. It is honest, insightful, and just disruptive enough to spark the kind of conversations higher ed needs right now. Bart encourages leaders to "Be curious. Be critical. Be willing to learn," and that theme runs through every chapter. What I appreciate most is that he never pretends to have all the answers. Instead, he helps leaders ask better questions. He brings experience, humility, and just enough humor to keep you turning pages. Higher ed leaders need this book. It is written with heart, clarity, and the kind of real experience that helps people and institutions move forward. Knowing Bart, every chapter was written with genuine care for the people he serves."

—HARRISON "SOUP" CAMPBELL, VP, Ardeo

"A must read for any leader in higher education, especially for those wanting to position marketing as a strategic leader for their university. Bart does an amazing job diving into the complexity of the state of higher education marketing but also tying in clear action items that you can take and implement immediately for your university."

—STEVEN RUTT, CRO, Abilene Christian University

"Bart Caylor hits a home run with this book. As a college president, I particularly appreciate Bart's clarity and innovation-forward approach to the marketing and enrollment imperatives we leverage as leaders. Because Bart appreciates the roles of president, board member, or other higher education stakeholders and decision-makers, his writing is easy to follow, making the complex digestible with particularly useful examples.

College presidents and all those engaged in leading higher education during this particularly dynamic era will benefit from his experience and wisdom. Actionable insights result from his synthesis and keen understanding of this particularly change-maddened time of higher education. Bart's hands-on understanding of contemporary complexities of not just marketing, but the entirety of higher education makes this a compelling read.

I used to be worried when my students told me they were ready for the test—no problem. They didn't know what they didn't know. Now, as leaders in this expanding and dynamic universe of higher education, we can really be ready for our rest. We can lead with confidence and insight into this evolving landscape of marketing and enrollment so vital to our missions and their future."

—RICHARD LUDWICK, President Emeritus, St. Thomas University

KNOW WHAT YOU DON'T KNOW

KNOW WHAT YOU DON'T KNOW

What Every Higher Ed Leader Needs
to Understand About Marketing

BART E. CAYLOR

THE
Higher
Ed
MARKETER
PRESS

Know What You Don't Know: What Every Higher Ed Leader Needs to Understand About Marketing
Published by The Higher Ed Marketer Press
Indianapolis, Indiana, U.S.A.

CAYLOR, BART E., Author
KNOW WHAT YOU DON"T KNOW
BART E. CAYLOR

Library of Congress Control Number: Print LCCN : 2025923894

ISBN: 979-8-9897639-6-2 KWYDK - Paperback KDP
         979-8-9897639-7-9 KWYDK - Paperback Ingram
ISBN: 979-8-9897639-8-6 KWYDK - Hardcover
ISBN: 979-8-9897639-5-5 KWYDK - Kindle ebook

Ghostwriter: Danielle Harward, Alliance Ghostwriting
Author Photo: Bart Caylor with Nano Banana
Publishing Management: Zach Coffin, The Higher Ed Marketer
Book Design: Heidi Caperton
Set in Adobe Caslon Pro 11pt

*To the colleagues and friends
in higher education
who have influenced my life and work.*

CONTENTS

INTRODUCTION: KNOW WHAT YOU DON'T KNOW

HAVE YOU HEARD OF APOLLO 13? It was the seventh crewed mission in NASA's Apollo space program, and it was intended to be the third mission to land astronauts on the Moon.[1] Ron Howard's movie classic, starring Tom Hanks, Bill Paxton, Ed Harris, and Kevin Bacon did a great job of telling the story. But, for those of you who haven't seen the movie, here is what you need to know.

In 1970, just two days into their mission, the crew of Apollo 13 experienced an onboard explosion that crippled their spacecraft and threatened their lives. Oxygen levels were dropping. Power was limited. The mission to land on the moon was scrapped. Now the only goal was survival.

Back on Earth, NASA's engineers at mission control were faced with a seemingly impossible task. They had to fix the spacecraft from *two hundred thousand* miles away, using only the materials available onboard.

They didn't have time for theory. They didn't have extra tools or unlimited budget. Instead, they dumped the contents of the spacecraft (things like duct tape, tubing, plastic bags, cardboard) onto a table so they could physically understand and interact with the tools they had to work with. Through relentless collaboration and creativity, they engineered a solution that brought the astronauts safely home.

You are in a similar situation: your institution is struggling. You likely won't raise a billion dollars or get approval for a massive new staff tomorrow. You may not have the perfect tools or all the time you'd like. But you still have a mission to complete. You have to attract the right students, guide your institution forward, and create results in a world that's changing fast. To do that, you'll need to be just as resourceful, strategic, and creative as those engineers, working with what you already have on the table.

Just like the Apollo 13 crew, and the engineers on earth, you face all sorts of challenges. Leading higher ed marketing today feels like aiming at a moving target. Everything around us is changing—technology, generational trends, expectations from students, and even the number of students coming through the pipeline. No wonder higher ed leaders and marketing teams feel stretched thin! As a leader, you likely feel pressure to innovate and deliver results. Yet, amid constant change, the real challenge is knowing what to ask, and when.

The problem is often not one of capability but of literacy. You don't have to know everything about marketing to be a good leader and get results. You don't have to be an expert in SEO, digital ads, or artificial intelligence. That's not your job. But if you're leading a team, you do need to know enough about these things to *ask the right questions*. That's where many leaders fall short—they don't know what they don't know.

If that sounds familiar, you're not alone. One of the biggest barriers I've seen in my thirty-five plus years working with higher ed leaders is that many are hesitant to admit they don't understand something. Maybe it's ego. Maybe it's fear of looking uninformed. Or maybe, in the rush to manage so many priorities, marketing was delegated before there was time to build a strong foundation. Whatever the reason, the result is the same. Decisions get made (or avoided) without the knowledge needed to ensure those decisions are sound.

This lack of marketing literacy often creates a vicious cycle, one that's easy to fall into and hard to recognize while you're in it. You don't fully understand a particular area of marketing, so you assume someone else does. You hand off the responsibility, trusting that your team, agency, or consultant knows what they're doing. And they might, but without a basic understanding of the landscape yourself, it becomes nearly impossible to evaluate their decisions, challenge assumptions, or make informed calls when something doesn't feel right.

When results stall or strategies underperform, you don't have the insight to troubleshoot. Instead, frustration builds. You might wonder if you hired the wrong person, chose the wrong platform, or simply don't have enough budget to compete. Meanwhile, your team may be just as confused or overwhelmed while doing their best, but don't have the strategic guidance they need.

That's when the blame game starts. You might find yourself saying, "We just need more staff," or "Marketing never works for us anyway," or "Our budget wasn't big enough," or "I assumed they knew what they were doing." But these aren't solutions. They're symptoms of a deeper problem. If you don't understand what you're leading, you can't lead it well. Don't get me wrong. Delegation is important, and leaders can't be in the weeds all the time. But if you are going to lead your team effectively, you need to know enough to engage in meaningful conversations, challenge assumptions, and steer the ship.

This book is not about turning you into a marketing expert. It's your guide to "knowing enough to know what you don't know" so you can ask the right questions.

We will cover several basics in marketing, including how to leverage AI, how to home in on a specific generation, how to understand key metrics of digital marketing, and much more. But we won't stop at technical knowledge. Leadership today requires more than knowing the right tools and strategies. It demands agility and adaptability. The world of higher education is changing fast, and the leaders who succeed will be those who can pivot, learn, and innovate in the face of uncertainty. Like those engineers on the ground, your strength isn't in knowing everything. It's in being able to work the problem. I'll teach you the foundational knowledge required to ask the right questions so you can better guide the strategy behind your marketing efforts.

I've spent the past three decades working at the intersection of higher education, marketing, and leadership. I've consulted with institutional presidents, cabinet members, marketing and enrollment teams, and marketing directors. I've seen firsthand the challenges they face and the strategies that work. Through my firm, Caylor Solutions, we've helped countless institutions elevate their marketing efforts and drive results. I've also had the privilege of engaging with leaders across the country through *The Higher Ed Marketer Podcast* where I've interviewed presidents, administrators, and marketing professionals to learn from their successes and struggles. And I've been recognized as one of the higher ed marketers to follow on social media.

All this to say, my experiences have given me a front-row seat to the challenges that higher education leaders navigate daily. But it's also given me the tools and mindsets that can help.

The enrollment cliff is no longer a distant concern—it's here. Fewer students means more competition, tighter budgets, and tougher decisions. And now, another challenge is emerging: the "search cliff." As more institutions go test-optional, fewer students are taking standardized tests like the ACT and SAT, meaning the traditional strategy of buying student names for outreach is drying up. The old methods of building your funnel are eroding, just as students themselves are becoming more discerning.

As a leader, you can't afford to rely on "the way we've always done things." The world has shifted, and higher education must shift with it. That means understanding the basics of digital marketing, knowing how to reach and resonate with today's students, and being willing to adapt and innovate when faced with unexpected challenges.

That's the Apollo 13 mindset. Work the problem. Use what you've got. Lead with clarity. You don't have to do it alone. You don't need every answer. You just need to uncover what you don't know and learn how to ask smarter questions. That's where we're headed.

1

TRUST, BUT VERIFY

"The important thing is not to stop questioning.
Curiosity has its own reason for existing."
—Albert Einstein

RONALD REAGAN ONCE SAID, "Trust, but verify." He used it in the context of diplomacy during the Cold War, specifically in arms control negotiations with the Soviet Union.[2] On the surface, it's a pithy line about the balance between confidence and caution. But Reagan didn't stumble onto that phrase.

He was introduced to it by Suzanne Massie, a scholar of Russian history who had advised him that Russians often speak in proverbs, and that learning a few would go a long way in building rapport with Soviet leaders. Massie suggested *doveryai, no proveryai*—"trust, but verify." Drawing on his background as an actor, Reagan practiced saying it in Russian, committed it to memory, and used it repeatedly in both private discussions and public statements. He understood that learning even a small part of the language would establish credibility and help him lead with more influence.

That same principle applies to you as a higher ed leader. You don't need to be fluent in marketing jargon, but you do need to understand enough of the language to engage meaningfully, challenge ideas when necessary, and verify the strategies being proposed or implemented. When you don't, you risk trying to lead without the right context or vocabulary.

Effective leadership means striking the balance between trusting your team's expertise while verifying the strategy, data, and direction. That requires literacy, not mastery.

You don't need to become a marketing expert, but you do need to have enough working knowledge to lead effectively. That means knowing enough about the topic to ask good questions and noticing when something doesn't sound right. And yes, it does mean trusting your team, but that trust can't be blind. When leaders don't understand the work well enough to ask the right questions or when they're too busy—or too hesitant—to admit what they don't know, that's when problems slip through the cracks and solutions are required.

Think about it like being a general contractor. You might not be the one installing the plumbing, but you should know enough to say, "That doesn't look right," or "Walk me through how this works." The same goes for a general medical practitioner. They don't perform heart surgery, but they know enough to recognize when something's wrong and bring in a specialist. That's what leadership literacy in higher ed marketing looks like.

One of my clients, a college president, likes to joke, "Bart, I'm just a Shakespeare scholar. I don't know anything about marketing!" I appreciate the humility. But I always remind him not to sell himself short. You don't need to be an expert. But you do need to be engaged. I've seen too many leaders fall into one of two camps: either they trust too much and stay hands-off, or they try to control everything but don't really understand what's going on. Neither extreme is sustainable.

The best leaders find a balance. They stay curious, and they develop enough understanding to lead with confidence, even when the landscape is constantly changing. This book is here to help you do that.

THE LOST ART OF LEARNING HOW TO LEARN

There was a time when leaders were expected to be well-rounded. Many came from a liberal arts background, an educational approach that emphasized big-picture thinking, intellectual curiosity, and moral character. The goal wasn't just to produce technical experts, but adaptable thinkers who could connect ideas across disciplines, ask insightful questions, and respond to complex challenges with wisdom. We taught learning as a *lifelong* skill, not just a means to a job.

While many institutions have shifted focus, some colleges still carry this torch. Institutions like Hillsdale College and the University of Dallas have doubled down on a liberal arts tradition rooted in classical texts, critical thinking, and the cultivation of virtue.[3] They represent a smaller but passionate movement that believes in educating not just for a career, but for life.

But as the landscape of higher education has shifted, so have its priorities.

In response to increasing pressure from the market, many areas of higher education have leaned hard into specialization. Parents want to see a clear return on investment. Students are asking, "Will this degree get me a job?" Institutions are competing to offer scholarships and outcomes that align with employer demand. As a result, some universities now reward hyper-specialization, pushing students to go deep into a single field as quickly as possible.

There's value in that, of course. Expertise matters. But there's also a risk. When we focus too narrowly, we lose the ability to see across disciplines, ask broader questions, and make the kinds of connections that spark innovation. We train people to become experts in one area, but sometimes at the cost of big-picture thinking. That same pattern shows up in leadership too. When leaders stay in their silos, they may miss warning signs—or opportunities—that lie just outside their expertise.

I'm not saying we need to go back to Socratic debates in every meeting. But we do need to recapture some of that curiosity and broad-minded literacy in our leadership today. Leaders don't need to be experts in everything, but they do need to be learners. They need to understand the landscape of the work their teams do well enough to engage meaningfully and lead wisely.

Comedian Nate Bargatze has a bit where he imagines going back in time to the 1920s, fully armed with everything he knows today. You'd think that would make him a revolutionary figure, but instead, he jokes, "I don't think I would make a difference." He imagines telling someone about smartphones and the internet, only to get tripped up by the first follow-up question: "How do they do it?" His answer? "Phew... I don't know how they do it. I think it's a satellite?" Then, of course, the next question comes: "What's a satellite?" At which point he panics and backpedals, saying, "I shouldn't have even said that... Uh... metal? Metal's gotta go pretty high in the air, I think?"

The joke lands because most of us can relate. We rely on powerful tools every day, but if pressed, we'd struggle to explain how they actually work. Bargatze even jokes that he couldn't prove he was from the future. He says, "They'd want to know who the next president is, and I'd say something like, 'Oh boy... uh...'" His delivery is hilarious, but the underlying truth is that we live surrounded by complex systems we depend on but barely understand.

That's why learning how to learn matters so much today. You don't need to become an expert in every function or technology. But you do need to recapture the curiosity, adaptability, and interdisciplinary awareness that once defined well-rounded leadership. We live in a time of amazing tools, technology, and opportunities. But if you're leading a team responsible for using those tools, you can't just shrug and say, "I don't know how it works." You need to understand enough about it to lead the people who utilize it.

STOP OUTSOURCING WHAT YOU'RE RESPONSIBLE FOR

Learning is a funny thing. We often expect it from others, but we forget to demand it from ourselves.

In higher education, we push for learning in our students. We talk about digital fluency, critical thinking, and even AI readiness. But when it comes to our own leadership, especially in unfamiliar areas like emerging technologies, new strategy, or evolving marketing methods, many of us quietly hand over the responsibility. We assume someone else (usually an external vendor) will figure it out.

The problem is when you outsource your learning, you also outsource your leadership. You can't lead what you don't understand. Take generative AI, for example. There's a lot of noise and confusion right now about how tools like ChatGPT fit into higher education. Should we embrace it? Regulate it? Ban it? For many leaders, the default response has been to defer to IT. And while your IT team is critical, this isn't just a technology issue. It's a leadership one.

The same pattern shows up in other areas too. I recently saw this in an institution's Financial Aid office. On the surface, everything looked fine. But something didn't sit right, so I called in a trusted enrollment expert to take a closer look. What she found was a broken process, a "set it and forget it" system that had quietly been costing the institution millions of dollars a year and hurting their yield. The staff wasn't lazy, and there were no bad intentions here; this mistake came down to lack of visibility. Leaders had handed off the responsibility years ago and assumed it was running smoothly.

We see this in digital advertising as well. It's an area many leaders are quick to hand off. The terminology sounds foreign. The dashboards are overwhelming. So, it gets outsourced. But when digital advertising teams talk about a "conversion," they usually mean someone clicked on an ad. That's it. In most other areas of marketing, a conversion means someone actually showed interest, like filling out a form or requesting more information. It's a small difference in language, but it can lead to big misunderstandings if you're not clear on what's really being measured.

Web strategy is another area that gets brushed aside. Leaders are more comfortable with print ads, brochures, or billboards because these are the channels they've known for decades.

The digital realm feels murky by comparison, so it's often under-funded, misunderstood, or delegated without oversight.

This all happened because leadership didn't know what they didn't know. But higher ed today can't afford that kind of distance. Whether it's AI, financial aid, or marketing strategy, these aren't just operational issues, they're leadership ones.

We've been here before. Higher ed isn't the first sector to feel overwhelmed by rapid innovation or unsure of how to lead through it. This moment reminds me of the early days of personal computing. Back then, computers were for hobbyists or people who hung out in RadioShack[4] and knew how to code. If you didn't speak the language of the disk operating system (DOS[5]), you were locked out. Most people, including educators and administrators, didn't engage with computers because they didn't feel equipped to.

Then along came Steve Jobs[6] and Steve Wozniak,[7] who believed technology should be accessible to everyone, not just the tech elite. With Apple, they introduced a computer you could use without knowing code. You could point. You could click. Suddenly, computers were for teachers, artists, writers, and yes, even higher ed administrators.

As a kid, I watched a neighbor boot up their machine by typing in lines of code. It seemed impossibly complicated. Then I discovered a Macintosh,[8] where all I had to do was click an icon, and it worked! That changed everything. It made technology approachable, and it was the system I learned on. This is the type of change we are currently experiencing today.

Generative AI is our modern-day Macintosh. Tools like ChatGPT don't require a background in computer science to use. They don't require coding. They don't even require calling the IT department. If you can use a smartphone or a browser, you can use AI. And yet, many leaders still treat these tools like they're outside their jurisdiction. But when we blindly defer to IT (or anyone else), we miss opportunities to lead.

If your institution's digital presence is your front door (and let's be honest, it is), you can't afford to look away. Students are forming opinions about your institution based on what they see online, and not just on your website. Take ZeeMee,[9] for example. It's a social platform designed specifically for prospective students, where they connect, share experiences, and talk about the institutions they're considering. ZeeMee includes pages for every college and university in the U.S., and students are having unfiltered conversations about your institution there whether you're paying attention or not. Yet, many higher education leaders have never even heard of it! It's a digital and generational blind spot *and* a missed opportunity for meaningful engagement.

If you don't understand what students are seeing, where they're seeing it, or how it's being measured, then you're not truly leading that part of your strategy.

I don't bring this up because I want you to become an expert in tech, marketing, or the details of enrollment or accounting. That's not your responsibility as a leader. But the digital world isn't going away. Neither is AI. Neither are shifting student expectations, evolving communication channels, or the demand for data-informed strategy. You don't have to know every detail about how these work, but you *do* need to know enough to lead the people who do. That means asking the right questions, understanding the vocabulary, and staying engaged, even when it's unfamiliar.

DON'T CONFUSE CONFIDENCE WITH COMPETENCE

One of the biggest mistakes I see in higher education marketing and leadership is assuming that titles equal expertise.

Just the other day, I asked an institution about their website strategy, which in my view was missing the mark dramatically. The IT director confidently told me they had optimized the site for SEO, which, on the surface, sounded great. But then he added, "That's why we didn't include very many pictures." That's right, very minimal use of images, no student stories, and no visual appeal. There was no emotion. The website was technically optimized for search engine robots, but not for actual students.

What's striking is that this approach likely made perfect sense to previous leadership. They heard "SEO," trusted that it was being handled, and never dug deeper. They didn't question whether that strategy truly aligned with student behavior or institutional goals because they hadn't taken the time to understand what SEO really means. Without that basic understanding, flawed strategies went unchallenged.

That kind of thinking misses the whole point of SEO. It's not just about following technical guidelines or making Google happy. It's about making sure your mission-fit students can actually find what they're looking for and have a good experience once they do. If your site shows up in search results but doesn't resonate or make sense when someone lands on it, you haven't really optimized anything. You've just made it easier for students to click away. And often, this happens because we're relying on the wrong kind of expertise.

Deferring to people who sound like they know what they're doing (especially when it comes to tech or marketing) is a common trap in higher education. Just because they speak the language, hold a certain title, or can throw around jargon doesn't mean they understand how to build strategy. It reminds me of watching piano "hacks" on social media. These videos teach you how to play a few easy chords with your left hand and match them with simple patterns on your right. If you break up the chords and stick to the right keys, it looks like you really know what you're doing. But really, you've learned a trick, not the instrument.

In the same way, someone might know how to run a Google ad, but do they understand your institution's enrollment goals? Your brand identity? Your mission-fit student? Asking questions helps surface those gaps early. When expectations are clear and goals are shared, collaboration becomes a lot more effective and a lot less frustrating down the line.

I've worked with marketing and leadership teams who later regretted a hire or a vendor partnership because the person they hired looked better on paper than they performed in reality. It's easy to be dazzled by buzzwords. It's harder to verify the real skill behind them.

This will only get trickier in the age of generative AI. With tools that can write content, generate designs, and even fake portfolios, it's more important than ever to vet people thoroughly. Ask to see real work. Ask for references. Talk to past clients. Don't be afraid to dig deeper. At Caylor Solutions, most of our work comes from word of mouth. Why? Because relationships build trust faster than credentials do. When a client recommends us to someone else, that credibility transfers immediately. That's why I'm a big believer in hiring and partnering through trusted networks.

When possible, work with people who come recommended. When that's not possible, take the time to vet them. Look them in the eye and ask real questions. Can they walk you through what they've done before? Do they listen as well as they speak? Do they have results to back up what they claim they can do for you?

Sometimes, even well-meaning people don't realize there's a gap. I've been on calls where vendors and clients are saying two completely different things but neither of them realize it. The vendor thinks they're selling brand awareness. The client thinks they're buying lead generation. Both parties believe they're aligned until the results come in and no one's happy.

Often, these moments are just miscommunication and not indicative of ulterior motives. But as the leader, it's your job to bridge that gap. To clarify expectations. To confirm deliverables. To ask, "What exactly are we buying?" and "How will we know if it's working?" Because if you don't ask those questions, you'll fill in the blanks with assumptions. And we've all heard that famous warning about what happens when you assume.

WHAT TO EXPECT IN EACH CHAPTER

Each chapter in this book is designed to build your understanding across key areas of higher education marketing and leadership. My goal is to give you the foundational knowledge and the right questions to ask so you can lead confidently in an increasingly complex world.

Here's a quick preview of what's ahead:

Chapter 2: Marketing with AI—Switching from Typewriters to Word Processors

We'll explore the fast-evolving world of generative AI. You'll learn how tools like ChatGPT can be your ally (not your replacement) and why an understanding of the technology matters.

Chapter 3: Marketing for Generations— 👍 = Passive Aggressive

Communication styles and platforms shift with every generation. This chapter breaks down how to market effectively across age groups, from Gen Alpha and Z students to Millennial parents to Gen X and Boomer alumni.

Chapter 4: Marketing Does Not Equal Advertising

Too many leaders equate marketing with promotions and ads. We'll unpack the full scope of marketing and show how to align your message with what students actually need.

Chapter 5: Marketing Programs—How Do I Sell Something Nobody Wants to Buy?

Not every program has a market. You'll learn how to evaluate demand, align programs with what students want, and make data-informed decisions about which programs to prioritize.

Chapter 6: Digital Marketing—$1,200 on a Keyword!?

We'll demystify the world of paid digital advertising. From PPC terms to budget strategy, you'll gain enough knowledge to spot red flags and avoid wasting money.

Chapter 7: Website Marketing—
Your Website Is Not a Catalog

Your website should engage and convert, not just inform. This chapter helps you turn your site into an enrollment tool with student-centered messaging and conversion-friendly design and move away from a transactional online brochure.

Chapter 8: Persona Marketing—You Are Not the Audience

You're not marketing to your board, your boss, or yourself. You're marketing to prospective students and their influencers. We'll show you how to build personas that reflect your audience and guide smarter strategies.

Chapter 9: Enrollment Marketing—
A Ferrari Can't Pull a Boat

Not every strategy transfers. We'll map out the enrollment funnel, talk about stealth applicants, and offer tactics for building a team that drives enrollment.

Chapter 10: Brand Marketing—Be a
Zebra in a Herd of Horses

Standing out starts with understanding your unique value. Learn how to craft a differentiated brand that boldly stands out in a crowded market.

Chapter 11: Marketing Through
Leadership—Think Like a CEO

Great marketing starts at the top. We'll explore what it means to lead like a modern CEO, where marketing, customer service, and sales all intersect, and why that mindset matters.

Chapter 12: Data-Driven Marketing—
The Rise of the Co-Bots

You don't need to be a data analyst, but you do need to know what questions to ask. This chapter introduces an approach to data that helps you get smarter insights, faster.

Chapter 13: Courageous Leadership

Being a higher ed leader today takes guts. This chapter explores how to challenge the status quo, make bold decisions, and lead with both heart and backbone, even when it's unpopular.

As you can see, I've filled this book with practical insights to help you grow your understanding, ask better questions, and lead your institution more effectively. You don't know what you don't know. But by reading this book, you'll learn the key concepts that will help you ask smarter questions and make better decisions.

Before you turn the page, I want to offer you a challenge. Approach this book with an open mind and a willingness to be honest with yourself, your team, and your institution. Be honest about what you know. But more importantly, be honest about what you don't know.

You don't need to have it all figured out. No one does. But if you bring your humility and a genuine desire to learn, this book will meet you right where you are.

In the following chapters, I'll also include a "take action" section filled with reflective questions and action steps to help you put what you've learned into practice in your own institution. These aren't about arriving at the one "right" answer—because as my college marketing professor, Dr. Michael Wiese says, "In marketing, rarely is there a right answer, but there's a right set of questions that lead you to a good answer." That line has stuck with me, and it's the essence of this book. You don't have to be an expert in every area to lead well; you just need to know enough to ask the right questions.

I was reminded of this recently while reviewing a school's IT budget. Something about the way they were paying for servers felt off to me. I admitted to my IT specialist that I had asked to validate my suspicions that I wasn't an expert, but I wanted to understand. He smiled and said, "You might not be an expert, but you know enough to notice when something doesn't add up. If you see smoke, there might be fire." That simple validation was powerful. Leadership doesn't mean having all the answers, but it does mean having the awareness and courage to ask the questions that uncover them.

That's what these reflection prompts are designed to do. You can answer them yourself or bring them to your team. It's your choice. But I will say, the more you get your team engaged in this book and the action steps I recommend within, the faster you'll gain buy-in for the changes your institution might need to make.

As you move through the next chapters, I encourage you to lean into curiosity. Take notes. Highlight the pages. Reflect on where you've been hands-off and where you need to re-engage. Show up with the mindset of a leader who's willing to grow. The challenges in higher education aren't getting easier. But you're not alone in facing them, and you're more capable than you think.

Let's get started.

2

MARKETING DOES NOT EQUAL ADVERTISING

"People don't buy the thing. They buy what the thing will do for them. In order for them to do that, you have to tell them a story. That story is a value story."

—Kindra Hall, *Stories That Stick*

A FEW YEARS AGO, I was brought in to work with an institution that had been seeing steady enrollment declines. The pressure was mounting. Leadership knew they had to do something to turn things around, and the board was pushing for a bold move to get in front of more prospective students.

So, they had done what many institutions in their position do, and they launched a massive regional TV ad campaign. The institution invested a significant portion of its marketing budget into television spots, professional production, and a media buy that would ensure their message reached households across the region.

The ads themselves were polished. They showcased sweeping drone shots of campus, smiling students walking across manicured lawns, and a voiceover highlighting the institution's academic excellence and long-standing reputation. The creative team checked all the boxes, and the institution looked prestigious and welcoming. For months, the ads aired across multiple stations and leadership was proud of the work. They believed that if more people knew about the institution, enrollment would naturally follow.

Except—it didn't. When the campaign ended, the institution had indeed gained name and brand recognition, but that was about it. Inquiries barely moved, applications didn't rise, and enrollment remained stagnant. The board was baffled. They had just spent *six figures* on advertising. The campaign looked great. Why hadn't it worked?

It didn't work because *marketing isn't just advertising*. Before I can give you the in-depth information needed on the different aspects of marketing, we have to start with this understanding as the foundation. A flashy campaign might make an institution more visible, but visibility alone doesn't drive enrollment. I've lost count of the number of times I've heard something like, "We don't need to market. If people know us, they'll come." Or, my personal favorite, "Marketing? Oh, you mean advertising."

One of the most common misconceptions in higher education is that marketing and advertising are the same thing. Many institutions believe that as long as they run ads—whether it's digital, print, or even a billboard—they've done their marketing. Others assume that advertising isn't necessary at all, thinking that if people know about them, they'll come.

This happens because advertising is the most visible aspect of marketing, so it's easy to assume that's all there is to it. But a marketing strategy that focuses only on advertising is like inviting people to a beautifully set dinner table and forgetting to prepare the meal. The real work happens before you ever launch an ad campaign.

THE FOUR PS OF MARKETING

Marketing is, at its core, about shaping how people perceive and engage with your institution. For this to happen, you need to understand your audience, shift their behaviors, and guide their decisions.

While advertising is a piece of marketing, it doesn't represent the whole picture. A great way to visualize where it fits into the plan comes from a popular social media meme that breaks down marketing into its key components. If you've spent time on TikTok or Instagram, you may have come across a post like the one the QR code to the right will take you to. In these types of posts, they explain marketing simply:[10]

- If you pay for a billboard, that's advertising.
- If a student hears about your institution from a friend, that's public relations.
- If your website helps a student compare financial aid options, that's content marketing.
- If you respond to a prospective student's DM on Instagram, that's customer service.

All of these are essential functions, but they each fall under the larger umbrella of marketing. Marketing is the strategy that *connects them all* and ensures they work together toward a common goal.

In the business world, marketing is understood through the Four Ps. These four elements—Product, Price, Place, and Promotion—represent the core areas businesses must align to attract and retain customers. Smart companies use the Four Ps as an integrated strategy. They evaluate each element through the eyes of their ideal customer and make adjustments based on market demand, competition, and behavior trends.

In higher education, we can apply the same lens:

- **Product**—What you offer. This includes not just academic programs, but the full student experience: campus life, extracurriculars, support services, and your institution's outcomes.

- **Price**—What it costs to attend. This goes beyond published tuition and includes perceived value, financial aid, scholarships, and even how transparent or complicated your pricing model feels to families.

- **Place**—Where and how prospective students interact with you. Is it on your website? Social media? High school visits? College fairs? This also includes the learning format—on-campus, online, or hybrid—and how accessible those channels are.

- **Promotion**—How you tell your story. This includes advertising, PR, social media, email campaigns, and the overall messaging that communicates your institution's value and mission-fit to your target audience.

Institutions are, at the end of the day, businesses. Like any business, they need to take a holistic approach to marketing if they want to succeed. If the product isn't what students need, the price isn't accessible, or the place isn't right, even the best promotional campaign will fail. Let's break down each of the Four Ps and explore how they impact marketing in higher education.

Product: Are You Offering What Students Actually Need?

The product in higher education is the education itself, including the programs, degrees, and experiences you offer. But for marketing to work, the product must be something people want and need.

Too often, I've been in meetings where institutional leaders decide they want to promote a new program simply because faculty believe it's valuable. No market research has been done. No one has asked whether prospective students are actually looking for this program or whether employers need graduates with these skills. In cases like this, institutions invest time and resources into launching and marketing a program that never gains traction.

In the realm of higher education, aligning academic offerings and experiences with market demand is crucial for institutional success. The legendary management consultant Peter F. Drucker once said, "The aim of marketing is to know and understand the customer so well the product or service fits him and sells itself."[11]

Before launching or promoting any program, leaders need to ask three critical questions:

1. Have we done market research?
2. Do we know the student persona for this program?
3. Have we talked to prospective students or employers to validate the need?

Market research doesn't have to be expensive. It can be as simple as organizing a focus group with current students and asking them about their interests and career goals. It could mean surveying potential employers to see if they would hire graduates from a new program. If you don't confirm demand for a program before launching it, you risk investing in something that won't attract students, no matter how much you promote it.

Price: Are You Communicating Cost Clearly and Competitively?

Price is one of the biggest barriers to enrollment, and yet many institutions fail to communicate it in a way that makes sense to prospective students.

Higher education has historically been insular in how it presents prices. Institutions think of price in terms of credit hours, but this is like selling a table by the square foot instead of just listing the price of the table.[12] If students can't quickly and clearly understand how much a degree will cost, they're more likely to walk away.

Additionally, in higher education, many institutions list inflated sticker prices, knowing that most students won't pay the full amount due to scholarships and financial aid. This is often referred to as the discount rate, hoping that there is a percentage of the prospective pool that can and will pay the full listed price. But prospective students and their families don't always know how to navigate this system, and many assume they can't afford college simply because they see an unrealistic price tag.

To address this, institutions should consider:

- Presenting price in a clear, digestible format. Some institutions are moving toward monthly tuition models, making it easier for students to budget.
- Ensuring the market can bear the price. If tuition is too high for your target audience, you need to either increase scholarships and funding or adjust costs to make it sustainable.
- Recognizing that price affects institutional structure. If you lower tuition, you may need to adjust overhead. With staff salaries making up 68% of an institution's budget, pricing decisions directly impact faculty and operations.

I've worked with several institutions[13] that have begun to rethink how they present pricing, especially for adult and non-traditional learners. In one case, an institution serving working adults experimented with shifting their tuition presentation to a monthly payment model.

Instead of listing the total per credit hour or per semester, they translated the cost into a monthly bill which was something their students were already used to budgeting for, like rent or a car payment. In response, they received increased engagement with their pricing pages and a higher rate of application starts. Even more importantly, this shift made the conversation about affordability feel more approachable, lowering the psychological barrier that often stops students from applying in the first place.

While pricing decisions typically fall outside of the marketing department, marketing leaders should still be involved in these conversations. If the price is too high for the market you're targeting, you need to raise that concern before launching a promotional campaign. We'll discuss this more in the next chapter, where I address the ever-rising question, "How do I sell something nobody wants?"

Place: Are You Meeting Students Where They Are?

If you are a mid-sized institution who launched an online MBA program, you might have the expectation that you would attract students nationwide. Leadership might even agree and seek to allocate a large portion of their budget towards broad, national digital ad campaigns.

But usually, after the first year, the numbers tell a different story. Most applicants still come from within a 200-mile radius. In fact, according to the Online College Students 2019 report,[14] 67% of fully online students now enroll in institutions located within just 50 miles of where they live, which is up from 42% just five years prior. Meanwhile, the number of students studying 100 miles or more from their chosen institution has dropped by more than half. This data reinforces that online is increasingly local. No matter how flexible or accessible online learning becomes, students still tend to choose institutions with regional familiarity, employer recognition, or personal connection.

I've seen this scenario play out repeatedly because universities assume that simply having an online program will make them a national player, but they hadn't considered the role of *place* in a student's decision-making process. This is why defining your place in terms of geography and how students engage with your institution is critical. If you're not meeting students where they are, both physically and digitally, you risk losing them to institutions that are.

Instead of marketing an online program as "accessible to students nationwide," institutions should consider leaning into their geographic strengths. Highlight partnerships with local businesses and industries that give students a career advantage. Showcase success stories of graduates working in the region to reinforce their impact. Or offer hybrid learning experiences and optional in-person events that create a sense of community.

When considering place, ask yourself:

- Are you positioning your institution as a local partner for workforce development? If so, your programs and pricing should reflect the needs of your regional job market.
- Are you preparing students for a specific community or cultural role? Faith-based institutions, for example, may be focused on shaping students for leadership in the church.
- Are you marketing to students in a place where they're actually looking? Are you seeking the correct watering holes?

Once you've defined who you serve and where, you can focus on ensuring your marketing strategy reaches students in those specific places.

Promotion: The Final Step, Not the First
Promotion is what most people think of when they hear the word "marketing." It includes advertising, social media, public relations, and all the other ways institutions try to get their

name in front of prospective students. And while visibility is important, promotion is only effective when it's done with a clear strategy that speaks to the right audience, at the right time, in the right way.

You could have the most well-executed marketing campaign with top-tier ad-creative expertly crafted messaging and a robust digital strategy, but if:

- The product isn't aligned with student needs,
- The price isn't competitive or transparent, or
- The place isn't accessible,

Then the best marketing in the world won't deliver results.

Many institutions assume they can promote their way out of a problem. They think that if they just run more ads, get more billboards, or spend more on digital campaigns, their enrollment challenges will disappear. But without addressing the fundamental issues of product, price, and place, promotion is just noise.

Unfortunately, however, marketing teams are often only brought to the table to discuss promotion, rather than being involved in conversations about what is being offered, how it's priced, and where it's positioned. This is a critical oversight. If marketing leaders were involved earlier in the decision-making process, institutions could avoid launching programs that students aren't searching for, pricing themselves out of their own market, or failing to reach the right audience in the right place.[15]

I've worked with institutions that offer criminal justice degrees, but the faculty decided to name the program "Administrative Justice." Their reasoning was valid: they felt it was a more accurate description of the discipline. But from a marketing perspective, this was a disaster. Prospective students weren't searching for "administrative justice." They were searching for "criminal justice." The program was effectively invisible to the very students it was designed for. This is a key example of why marketing should be involved from the beginning of a new program so that the product, price, and place are cohesive and *enhance* the promotion strategy instead of taking away from it.

NOW, IT'S TIME FOR STORY

Once the Four Ps are aligned, the next step is to tell a compelling story. Storytelling is an ancient and powerful tool. It can move past logic and tap into emotion and imagination. It lets prospective students see themselves at your institution and the career they could have after attending.

Yet, I often see higher education marketing lean heavily on transactional content such as lists of features, steps to apply, tuition breakdowns, and deadlines. While this information is required, it doesn't inspire action on its own. What truly motivates students to choose a college or institution is the story of how this experience will shape, and benefit, their lives.

In *Storythinking*,[16] author Angus Fletcher argues that modern communication has become too rational, too transactional, and ultimately, too forgettable. Institutions often assume that if their programs are well-structured, affordable, and high-quality, students will naturally enroll. But logic alone doesn't inspire action—imagination does.

This is why the world's most beloved brands don't just sell products; they sell lifestyles. Nike sells a mindset of perseverance and excellence. Apple sells creativity and innovation. Similarly, higher education marketing shouldn't just be about degree programs and tuition rates, it should be about who students will become, the experiences they will have, and the life they can build by being part of your institution. When students can see their own story unfolding within your institution, choosing to enroll becomes an emotional decision, not just a logical one.

This is why I chose Kindra Hall's quote from her book *Stories that Stick*[17] at the beginning of the chapter. Facts and figures alone aren't enough to drive enrollment decisions. Prospective students need to see how attending your institution will improve their lives. Whether it's opening doors to career opportunities, expanding their network, or giving them the confidence to pursue their goals, you need to articulate the value you offer. When marketing relies solely on logic, it fails to ignite the emotional connection that compels people to take action.

Ask yourself:

- What will life be like for students who choose this institution?
- How will their careers be shaped by this experience?
- What kind of community will they belong to?

The more emotion and storytelling you incorporate, the more prospective students will begin to see themselves in your institution. For example, here is a transactional approach versus a storytelling approach to marketing an engineering program:

1. A transactional approach might say:
   "Our engineering program offers a rigorous curriculum, expert faculty, and cutting-edge technology. Students complete coursework in thermodynamics, circuit analysis, and materials science."

2. A storytelling approach might say:
    "When Olivia was in high school, she loved tinkering with machines but wasn't sure if she could turn that passion into a career. At [Institution Name], she found a supportive community, hands-on experience in world-class labs, and mentors who guided her every step of the way. Today, she's designing sustainable energy solutions for underserved communities."

Which of those examples is more likely to get a prospective student excited?

Storytelling invites students into a vision of their future. Luckily this shift doesn't require massive changes. It can be as simple as integrating real student stories, immersive imagery, and messaging that speaks to the heart of the educational outcome. By moving away from just facts and into a storytelling-driven approach, institutions can inspire students to take the next step because they *see themselves in the story being told*.

WEAVING STORYTELLING INTO YOUR MARKETING

Now that you understand the power of story, the next step is knowing how to use it effectively. Many institutions acknowledge that storytelling is important, but when it comes to execution, they revert to listing features and facts rather than creating compelling narratives.

At its core, storytelling is about more than just sharing student testimonials or alumni success stories. It's about shaping the entire way an institution presents itself and making prospective students feel something when they engage with your website, visit your campus, or see your promotional materials. Every touchpoint should contribute to a larger narrative, one that is emotional and immersive.

Here are a few key ways to bring storytelling into your marketing strategy:

1.   Help Students Envision Themselves in Your Programs

One of the biggest obstacles prospective students face is uncertainty. They wonder if they'll fit in, if they'll succeed, if this is truly the right place for them. That's why storytelling in marketing shouldn't just focus on what students will learn but also who they will be surrounded by and how they will find their place within the community.

What if your website was dedicated to telling this story within each of your programs? The introduction to a computer science program might start like this:

> *"When James first arrived at [Institution Name], he wasn't sure where he fit in. He knew he wanted to study computer science, but he worried about making friends and finding his place outside the classroom. That changed the moment he walked into his first hackathon event. He met students who shared his passion for technology, professors who took an interest in his ideas, and mentors who encouraged him to push his skills further. By the end of his first year, he was building apps with his classmates and collaborating on research with faculty. Today, James is leading an AI development team and mentoring students."*

When institutions use storytelling to highlight the friendships formed in study groups, the late-night brainstorming sessions in the library, or the moments of encouragement from a professor, they tap into the sense of belonging potential students crave. And that storytelling can take many forms, including text, video, student-led podcasts, Instagram takeovers, testimonials, and even digital storybooks. Whether it's a short clip of roommates laughing on move-in day or a parent reflecting on their child's graduation journey, each story brings the student experience to life in a different way.

The format matters less than the feeling it evokes. What counts is the authenticity and emotional resonance that helps prospective students picture themselves on your campus, surrounded by people who see and support them.

2. Use Imagery That Invites Imagination

Many universities rely heavily on images of empty buildings, aerial shots of campus, or meticulously staged photos of students posing for a brochure. While these types of visuals serve a purpose, they don't help a prospective student feel what it's like to be part of the community. Think about the difference between a photo of a grand lecture hall with no students in it versus a photo of a lively discussion happening inside that same hall. One feels cold and impersonal, the other feels dynamic and engaging.

Rather than showcasing still and lifeless images, institutions should focus on visuals that tell a story. A professor leaning over a student's desk, helping them with a project. A group of friends walking across campus laughing and engaged in conversation. A student standing proudly in their cap and gown, surrounded by family on graduation day.

These types of images invite prospective students to picture themselves in those exact moments. They offer a window into daily campus life, beyond the facilities, and help prospective students imagine themselves as part of the community.

3. Focus on the "Why" Behind Your Institution

Many institutions spend a lot of time communicating what they offer but fail to clearly articulate why they exist. When marketing becomes a collection of features and statistics, it loses the human element that makes a brand truly compelling. Instead of just listing programs and credentials, institutions should take a step back and think about their larger purpose.

- What kind of students do they want to develop?
- What impact do they want their graduates to have on the world?

Students don't just choose a college based on rankings, programs, or even cost, they choose based on their why. Every prospective student has a personal motivation driving their decision to pursue higher education. It could be a desire to break into a competitive field, a passion for a specific subject, the need for financial stability, or the hope of being part of something bigger than themselves. Institutions that focus solely on what they offer miss the opportunity to connect with students on a deeper level.

When an institution aligns its messaging with the why behind a student's journey, it creates a sense of purpose and belonging. It changes the decision from where should I go? into *where do I see myself growing and achieving my goals?*

Instead of saying, "We offer a rigorous curriculum in business administration," this could change to, "We develop future business leaders who will innovate and drive change in the global economy." Prospective students are choosing a mission that aligns with their own ambitions. So, you need to show them how, and why, you align with them too.

Remember, advertising is only part of the marketing umbrella. When you take the time to ensure that your product, price, and place are working together before diving into promotion, you stop chasing students and start attracting them. Then you infuse storytelling into your marketing, so your mission-fit students can see themselves thriving at your institution before they even apply.

TAKE ACTION

With an understanding of the four Ps of marketing and how you can use storytelling to enhance your message, you can take a critical eye to your current marketing incentives. The following exercises and reflection points are designed to help you apply the ideas from this chapter to your unique context. Take time to work through them, either on your own or with your team, and use them as a springboard for meaningful conversations and actionable insights.

Reflective Questions

- Do internal conversations about marketing focus mostly on promotion, or are product, price, and place also part of the discussion?
- Have there been times when an advertising campaign didn't produce the expected results? What factors— beyond just visibility—might have contributed to that outcome?
- Product: Is there a program or offering at your institution that struggles with enrollment? Have market research and student demand been taken into account?
- Price: Does your institution clearly communicate pricing and financial aid in a way that is easy for students and families to understand? Are there hidden costs that might create confusion or barriers to enrollment?
- Place: How are you reaching students where they are— both geographically and digitally? Are you assuming

online programs will attract students from anywhere, or are you considering regional influences on enrollment?

- Promotion: Are your marketing efforts telling a compelling story, or are they primarily transactional? Do students see themselves reflected in your messaging?
- Does your institution currently use storytelling in its marketing? If so, how effective is it versus your more technical marketing promotions?

Action Steps

- Audit your institution's marketing approach. Review your recent marketing materials such as ads, website content, brochures, and emails. Identify one area where your institution could strengthen its marketing approach by considering one of the other Ps more intentionally.
- Integrate market research into program development. If your institution is considering launching a new program, initiate a market research check. Gather data from prospective students, alumni, and employers to determine demand before moving forward. You can also use this strategy to identify problems in programs struggling with enrollment.
- Review how tuition and fees are presented on your website. Is it clear and easy to understand? Are prospective students and their influencers able to quickly determine what their actual cost will be without having to engage in the net price calculator?
- Map out where the majority of your students come from. If you have online programs, analyze whether

your marketing aligns with the reality that most students enroll from within a few hours of campus. Bonus points if you use ChatGPT. If your institution is heavily reliant on local students, explore ways to strengthen community partnerships to reinforce your institution's role in workforce development and regional growth.

- Identify a program page or marketing piece that is purely informational and rewrite it with a story-driven approach. Focus on who the student becomes as a result of the program.

- Choose one upcoming campaign and commit to leading with storytelling rather than statistics. Use student testimonials, alumni success stories, or faculty perspectives to illustrate the impact of your institution. Track engagement and responses. Do students engage more with story-driven content compared to purely promotional messaging? Use these insights to refine your approach going forward.

3

MARKETING WITH GENERATIVE AI: SWITCHING FROM TYPEWRITERS TO WORD PROCESSORS

"Good artists copy, great artists steal."
—Pablo Picasso

FOR NEARLY A CENTURY, the typewriter was the gold standard for writing. When it first came out, it was a tool that revolutionized communication and productivity. By the 1950s, electric typewriters made the process faster and more efficient, but they still adhered to the same basic principles. In fact, remember using one in high school. It was a hybrid between the typewriter and the word processor. It felt advanced at the time, a glimpse into the future. But by the time I got to college, typewriters were obsolete. Everyone was using software like WordPerfect or Microsoft Word to write papers and send documents.

However, not all of us made the transition easily. For many, the typewriter was reliable, familiar, and good enough. Learning a new system felt unnecessary, even daunting. But the world doesn't slow down for our comfort. Those who resisted the shift found themselves at a disadvantage, while those who embraced the new tools gained a competitive edge in productivity and innovation. Microsoft Word didn't just make typing faster; it introduced spell check, formatting, editing, and collaboration features that fundamentally changed how work got done. It gave users more control, more clarity, and more efficiency.

Today, we're standing at the edge of another shift: artificial intelligence. Just as the typewriter gave way to the word processor, AI is reshaping how we work, communicate, and lead. And much like before, there's resistance.

The hesitancy to embrace generative artificial intelligence isn't surprising. Many leaders are already stretched thin, managing tight budgets, enrollment challenges, and a constantly shifting higher education landscape. Adding "learn AI" to the to-do list can feel overwhelming. For some, the resistance comes from fear of being replaced, of making mistakes, or of not understanding how the technology works. For others, it's skepticism: Is AI really worth the hype? Then there are others, especially in educational institutions, whose first glimpse at AI was through the cheating papers of their students. That put a real chip on every academic's shoulder. Understandably so! But it doesn't mean we should refuse to allow AI into our lives.

AI isn't a passing trend or a flashy gimmick. It's a fundamental shift in how we operate. As a leader, you have a relationship with AI that sets the example for your team and the future you're building for your institution. Organizations adopt AI faster when their leaders adopt it first. And according to the Boston Consulting Group, companies that adopt AI quickly can claim 1.5x higher revenue growth than other companies![18]

When a leader uses AI tools, even in small ways, it signals to the team that this technology matters, that it's worth learning, and that it's here to stay. Conversely, when a leader encourages their team to use AI but avoids it themselves, they send a mixed message that says, "This is important for you, but not for me." That kind of disconnect undermines trust and slows progress.

Now you might be feeling like I tricked you into reading a chapter all about generative artificial intelligence. But the tools themselves aren't the point. Generative AI platforms will evolve, just as word processors and personal computers have. They will be different in the next few years than they are now and will continue evolving past that. What matters is the mindset with which you approach this new technology. Are you willing to step into the unknown, to experiment, and to learn alongside your team? Or will you cling to familiar processes while the world moves on around you?

The tools and strategies that worked in the past—whether it's a reliance on traditional marketing methods or a hesitation to adopt new technologies—won't carry us through the challenges ahead. The enrollment cliff is already here, reshaping the higher education landscape. Students today expect authenticity, personalized experiences, and seamless digital interactions. If we're going to meet those expectations, we need to think differently, act boldly, and embrace the tools that will help us iterate on old strategies.

This isn't about turning you into a generative AI expert or overwhelming you with technical jargon. It's about showing you why adapting to change more broadly is critical for your success as a leader. Throughout this book, you'll find practical strategies for using generative AI to enhance your efforts, whether it's streamlining workflows, analyzing data, or improving communication. But none of that will matter if you're not willing to take the first step required to get curious about what this technology can do for you and your team.

A NEW KIND OF ELECTRICITY

Every major shift in history has been met with resistance, and today's rise of generative AI is no exception. We're living through what some are calling the Fourth Industrial Revolution, which I discuss more in depth in the textbook chapter I authored in the 2025 marketing textbook *AI in Marketing*.[19] And yet, much like those earlier shifts, generative AI is often misunderstood, resisted, and dismissed.

Andrew Ng, one of the most influential voices in artificial intelligence, has often said that "AI is more like electricity than it is another tool."[20] His point is that just as electricity transformed every industry and became woven into daily life, AI will do the same across every sector of society. That analogy has been so compelling that other leaders, including Google's CEO Sundar Pichai and even policymakers, have echoed it in their own speeches.[21] Think about that. You don't flip a light switch and marvel at the mechanics of electricity. You just turn on the light and go about your business. I bet you don't even think about why or how it turned on! That's the future of AI. It will be everywhere, seamlessly integrated into how we work, communicate, and lead. We won't have to think about it. We will simply use it.

But for many in higher education, AI hasn't arrived as a tool for empowerment. It showed up in the headlines as a way for students to cheat. That's how many academic leaders were first introduced to it, and that framing stuck. Instead of seeing AI as a new opportunity to create more efficiency, they saw it as a shortcut, a way to cut corners. That initial reaction shaped how AI has been perceived by many today, but especially by leaders with deep academic roots.

This misunderstanding has led to a cascade of challenges. In my consulting work, I've seen institutions ban AI outright, viewing it as a threat rather than a tool. Others have handed the responsibility for AI adoption entirely to their IT departments, under the assumption that anything involving technology belongs solely in their hands. And perhaps most telling, one of the most common questions I hear isn't, "How can we use AI to solve our institution's biggest challenges?" but, "What's the best tool for detecting AI use?" (Spoiler: none of them really work.) That kind of question reflects a reactive mindset, more concerned with policing AI than exploring its potential.

This approach is holding institutions back. IT departments aren't designed to take risks or push boundaries; their role is to ensure stability and security. When decisions about AI are left solely to IT, many times it's not because of resistance, but because—like everyone else—they don't know what they don't know.

In more advanced and innovative IT environments, like at Arizona State University, AI is being embraced and explored as a strategic tool.[22] But for many small to mid-sized institutions, IT departments may lack the resources, exposure, or training to lead in this area. The result is often a cautious, narrowly scoped implementation that misses the broader potential of generative AI as a tool for creativity, personalization, and institutional transformation. Worse, this mindset reinforces the idea that generative AI is purely a technical issue, rather than a leadership opportunity.

That belief couldn't be further from the truth. Generative AI thrives in the hands of those who know how to take risks and think critically. It's a tool for creativity, innovation, and problem-solving, not just another piece of software to be plugged into a system. Every faculty, staff, and student should be taught how to utilize generative AI to the fullest of its ability for the empowerment of each person's subject matter expertise.

This resistance to AI reminds me of a conversation I had with my grandmother when I was in high school. I told her I was taking a typing class, and she laughed. "Why would you need to learn that?" She continued to say, "You're smart enough that you'll always have a secretary to do it for you!" Her comment came from a place of tradition, from an era when typing was considered a task for support staff, not a skill for leaders. But by the time I entered the workforce, typing wasn't optional. It was a basic skill everyone needed to succeed. If I had bought into that old way of thinking, I would have been left behind.

That's exactly what's happening with AI today. Too many don't see how deeply AI will be implemented in our lives in the near future. It will be the lightbulb we turn on so we can go about our day. It will enhance us, support us, and help us get more time back in our lives to do the things we love. It will shape every aspect of how we work and communicate.

I know the reluctance to embrace generative AI is rooted in our tendency to adapt new tools to old conventions rather than rethinking the conventions themselves. It's easier to fit AI into existing workflows than to imagine entirely new ways of operating. But if we're going to lead effectively in this new era, we need to let go of those outdated approaches and embrace the possibilities AI offers.

Generative AI has the power to revolutionize how we engage with students, analyze data, and make decisions. It can stream-line processes, enhance creativity, and uncover opportunities we might never have seen otherwise. But none of that will happen if we see AI as a shortcut or a threat.

EVALUATING EMERGING TECHNOLOGIES

Many think the challenge of emerging technologies is in understanding how they work. But there is an added layer to the challenge, and that is in assessing if they are right for you. Higher education leaders are skilled at thoughtful evaluation, but the rapid pace of innovation can make it difficult to apply that strength without intentional effort.

First, let's address the biggest obstacle: our assumptions. Too often, we approach new technologies with preconceived notions about what they are, how they should be categorized, or whether they fit into our worldview. In the previous sections of this chapter, I've given you several examples of these assumptions. Unfortunately, they often block us from accessing the true potential of emerging technologies.

Take generative AI, for example. It's not just about creating text or images; it's a pattern recognition and prediction tool. But because many higher education leaders were first introduced to AI through its misuse, there's a tendency to dismiss it outright as unethical or problematic. That initial impression has led some institutions to ban AI entirely, short-circuiting conversations about how it could be a game-changer for education and leadership. On top of that, many have made the argument that AI is "stealing" because it draws on existing data to create new content.

However, they say this without understanding the nuances of how AI works. In reality, AI learns by recognizing patterns, much like the great artists of the Renaissance learned by studying the masters before them. A classic example of learning through imitation is Pablo Picasso. Though widely known as one of the most innovative artists of the 20th century, Picasso was deeply rooted in tradition. From a young age, under the guidance of his father, he engaged in the disciplined practice of copying the masterworks, sketching plaster casts, and drawing live models. Picasso famously believed that artistic freedom could only come *after* mastering foundational techniques, even suggesting that every artist's studio should carry the sign École de dessin (drawing school) above their door[23]

And he wasn't alone. Leonardo da Vinci apprenticed under Andrea del Verrocchio, absorbing techniques like sfumato and building upon them. Peter Paul Rubens spent years copying Titian. Artists like Goya, Manet, van Gogh, and Matisse all followed this path as well—they started by studying the greats, mastering the rules, then breaking them.[24]

The parallel to AI is striking. Like these artists, AI systems learn by studying existing works. It recognizes patterns, emulates structure, and eventually generates something new. It's not mindless duplication. It's the same iterative, cumulative process that has always driven human creativity forward.

But let's step outside of AI for a moment, because we tend to make assumptions about *all* emerging technologies. Electric vehicles (EVs) have quite a few assumptions surrounding them. I've experienced this firsthand. I own an EV, and I've been labeled a "tree hugger" by people who assume my choice aligns with a broader set of political views. It doesn't. I made my decision based on research, practicality, and values that made sense for me. But those snap judgments on both sides are a perfect example of how quickly we try to fit technology into our existing belief systems.

The irony is that some people might not even recognize my EV at first glance. I drive an F-150 Lightning. It looks like a pickup. It hauls like a pickup. But it runs on electricity. In this way, it's also similar to generative AI because it doesn't always look the way people expect, and that gap between expectation and reality is where misunderstanding thrives.

This tendency to judge prematurely is where many leaders get stuck. Let me challenge you to stop making assumptions and quick decisions about new technologies. It's easy to yield authority to other "experts" and assume they'll know what's best, but they won't always understand your institution's unique needs.

Instead, take the time to critically evaluate new technologies. Start by asking three key questions:

1. What is the extent of this technology's capabilities?
2. How does it work?
3. How can it apply to what I need?

And don't stop there. Look at the technology from multiple perspectives. Talk to people with varying opinions, even those who think it's unethical or problematic. Listen to concerns, but don't let them dictate your decisions. Find others who use the technology consistently. What breakthroughs have they made? How has it made their life easier? Seeing both sides of the technology will allow you to make a fairer judgement of its worth.

This broader perspective matters. When you stop following the roar of the crowd and instead dig into the reality of a technology, you're no longer bound by popular misconceptions. You position yourself as a leader who can make a final decision about it with confidence and educate those around you as to why.

Leadership in this space also requires experimentation. New technologies often feel intimidating because we don't understand them yet. The best way to overcome that is to dive in, test it out, and try something new.

When I started working on websites, I didn't know HTML. I was a designer with some technical background but not enough to code a site from scratch. Then one day, in 1994, the programmer for our website build project (yes, our *first* website) backed out after the kickoff meeting (since he "didn't know HTML"). We were all hyped about the idea of getting a website, it had already been announced, and there was no backing out now! My boss suggested finding another programmer, but I didn't want to rely on someone else who might do the same thing. So, on the way home, I stopped at a bookstore, picked up a thin book on HTML, and read it cover to cover that night. I didn't even have access to a computer at home, so the next morning at work, I started experimenting, typing code into brackets and following the book's instructions. It was frustrating and time-consuming, but by the end, we had a functioning website.

The best way to learn is by doing. You don't need to master a technology before you try it, but you do need to be willing to step out of your comfort zone and engage with it. This applies to everything I'll explain in this book. You can read about methods, strategies, and tools, but to truly understand their value, you need to sit down with the experts, experiment, and figure out what works for you. Be curious. Be critical. Be willing to learn. That's how you lead in a world shaped by emerging technologies.

UNDERSTANDING HOW LARGE LANGUAGE MODELS WORK

Now that we understand how to address and evaluate new technology, let me get back on my AI soap box. Because we are entering the fourth industrial revolution, I need to dedicate some space in this chapter to unraveling the mysteries of large language models (LLMs) like ChatGPT and how they work. As humans, we tend to make sense of the unknown by comparing it to what we already know. But LLMs aren't like other tools we're familiar with, and that's where misconceptions arise.

Take Google, for example. It's tempting to think of LLMs as just another search engine because, on the surface, the experience looks similar: you type something into a box and get a response. But the way LLMs function is *fundamentally* different. Google is essentially a giant, highly organized library. When you ask it a question, it searches its database of indexed web pages and retrieves the most relevant information. It's pointing you to something that already exists.

LLMs don't work that way. They don't retrieve pre-existing information. Instead, they generate new content in real time. They do this by analyzing patterns they've learned from vast amounts of training data and predicting, in the case of text, what word, phrase, or sentence is likely to come next based on the input you provide. It's a bit like an improvisational actor who, instead of memorizing a script, knows the rules of storytelling so well they can make up dialogue on the spot that feels cohesive and intentional.

The same concept applies across media. For images, it's predicting the next pixel. For audio, the next sound wave. For video, the next frame. Even with numbers and data, it's about forecasting what comes next in the pattern. In every case, the engine behind the scenes is prediction, not memory.

LLMs also aren't copywriters—at least not in the way higher ed marketers might think. They can generate content quickly, but they lack the ability to truly understand context, emotion, or the nuanced needs of a specific audience. A skilled copywriter in higher education knows how to craft messaging that resonates with prospective students, speaks to their parents' concerns, and aligns with an institution's brand voice. LLMs don't have those instincts. They're tools to enhance creativity and efficiency, not replace the human touch.

At their core, LLMs are just highly advanced pattern predictors. They analyze enormous datasets—billions of words from books, articles, websites, and other sources—to learn how language works. Then, when given a prompt, they process it, predict the most likely sequence of words based on probabilities, and generate a response.

Arthur C. Clarke, an author famous for his short stories, captured this feeling perfectly in *Profiles of the Future* (revised 1973 edition) when he wrote, "Any sufficiently advanced technology is indistinguishable from magic."[25] To many people, LLMs feel like magic, but they're not. They're incredibly sophisticated machines built on algorithms that boil down to ones and zeros.

Understanding this distinction is critical because it clarifies what LLMs can and cannot do. For one, they aren't "thinking." They don't have ideas, opinions, or knowledge in the way humans do. They're not copywriters, and they're not a substitute for human creativity or expertise. What they do is generate content that mirrors the patterns they've learned, and they do it at astonishing speeds. Even the most advanced models aren't truly reasoning. They're just getting better at predicting what comes next.

This is where the comparison to a skilled higher ed marketer can help make sense of things. As a marketer, you rely on years of experience, training, and intuition to craft messaging that resonates with prospective students, parents, and stakeholders. You don't just write words; you connect with your audience on an emotional level, aligning your messaging with their needs and your institution's goals. An LLM doesn't do that. It lacks the understanding, empathy, and brand knowledge that you bring to the table. But it can enhance your work by speeding up brainstorming, generating drafts, or helping you explore creative directions you might not have considered. As we discuss in our AI training workshops, subject matter expertise is and will always be required.

This distinction is important because it shifts the conversation about AI from fear to opportunity. Many higher education leaders resist tools like LLMs because they seem like shortcuts. That framing has created a lasting skepticism, making it harder for leaders to see the real potential of AI. But the truth is, these tools aren't shortcuts or cheats. They're accelerators. They free up time by automating repetitive tasks, enhance creativity by offering new ideas, and make complex tasks like data analysis more accessible.

As Seth Godin put it in a recent interview, "If you did a job that uses electricity, and electricity was about to be very different, you could easily say, 'Electricity is going to steal all our jobs.' And in some ways, it did—cars replaced blacksmiths." But the more important question isn't *if* AI will change your work, it's *how*. Godin continues, "The short-term impact of AI is either an AI works for you, or you are competing with one. If you are competing with one, you've got trouble." He gives the example of radiology and how AI can now read X-rays more accurately than radiologists in 90% of cases. "If you're a radiologist," he says, "you don't want to be opposed to that. You want to be asking, 'How do I get AI to work for me so that I can become a different kind of radiologist?'"[26]

He continues to explain that the same goes for writers, stating that asking ChatGPT for twenty possible subtitles isn't cheating, it's smart. You still have to decide which one is best. The point he's making is even if you use these tools, it still requires your discernment and creative thinking. What AI does is eliminate the chore work so that human energy can be spent making decisions, asking better questions, and making meaningful connections. As Godin says, "If a chore can be profitably done by an AI, it will." The opportunity now is to shift our focus from what AI *does* to what it *frees us to do*.

TIPS TO MAKE PROMPTING YOUR SUPERPOWER

For years, I told people that AI was a tool. Useful, but ultimately just another program to add to their arsenal. While that's not untrue, I've come to realize that it's far more than that. AI isn't just a tool; it's a collaborator, a partner in creativity and problem-solving. The moment you stop thinking of AI as a program to command and start treating it like a knowledgeable resource with whom you can brainstorm and co-create, the experience shifts entirely. Prompting, when done right, can become your superpower.

The shift begins with mindset. Imagine hiring an intern. You wouldn't hand them a task without adequate and a thorough explanation, right? Instead, you'd outline your expectations, provide examples of what you're looking for, and explain the broader purpose behind the task. You would provide them with clarity and specifics. That's exactly how you should approach prompting AI. Instead of seeing it as a machine that requires precise instructions, treat it as a colleague. When you give it context, set parameters, and clarify your needs, you'll be amazed at the results.

I consistently see people selling a book of "100 Best ChatGPT Prompts for Marketing," but the best way to use an LLM is not with the perfect prompt. You'll find more success when you treat each interaction like a conversation. That is the very reason they call it "Chat"GPT.

Typically, I start with a broad idea or question, something simple like, "How can we make our scholarship campaign stand out to high school seniors?" The AI would respond with a list of ideas, and I'd follow up with refinements: "Focus on digital platforms, and include examples for TikTok and Instagram." From there, the AI would narrow its suggestions, and I could ask for more specific outputs, like, "Write a 30-second TikTok script based on idea three." Each interaction built on the last, and the result felt less like using a tool and more like brainstorming with a teammate. Our goal is to get 60 or 70 percent of the way there in a draft, fast. By using AI to handle the repetitive tasks that slow us down, we free ourselves up to focus on what really matters—being more creative, strategic, and effective in our work.

Providing context is key to unlocking this dynamic. The more specific you are, the better the results. If I'm drafting a newsletter, for example, I might upload an older example, explain the audience, and specify the tone I'm aiming for. The AI then has a frame of reference, which helps it deliver more aligned suggestions. Over time, as I've worked with tools like ChatGPT, I've realized that it's capable of recognizing patterns in our interactions. After months of use, I asked, "What have you learned about my preferences from our past conversations?" The insights were surprising and helpful, showing me nuances about my own style that I hadn't consciously identified.

The introduction of visual capabilities, like ChatGPT's Vision Mode, takes this collaboration even further. You can check out the video of me testing it out with the QR code on the right.[27] This opens up AI to all sorts of capabilities. You could upload an image of a campus tour flyer and ask, "What does this communicate to a prospective student? How would you improve it?" It can review the

flyer and suggest ways to make the design more compelling. It's incredible to think that AI can now "see" what you're working on and provide actionable feedback!

Great prompting creates great results. It allows you to work faster and more effectively than before. But great prompting starts with your mindset. I'd like to credit my colleague Zach Coffin, Vice President of The Higher Ed Marketer, who helped identify five essential mindset shifts that we teach in our AI classes: fear to curiosity, control to collaboration, perfection to catalyst, mystery to lifelong learning, and efficiency to enhancement. Each of these shifts plays a vital role in transforming how we approach generative AI and, more specifically, how we craft effective prompts.

The first shift, from fear to curiosity, includes much of what we have discussed already and creates the foundation for the other mindset shifts required. Many people view generative AI with skepticism, perceiving it as a potential threat to creativity, jobs, or even authenticity. However, reframing this fear into curiosity opens a world of possibilities. When you see generative AI not as a replacement for human ingenuity but as a tool for exploration, you unlock its potential.

The second shift, from control to collaboration, is about letting go of the need to micromanage every aspect of the creative process. In traditional workflows, we often strive for complete control over outcomes. With generative AI, the power lies in collaboration. Treat the AI as a partner that brings its own insights and ideas to the table. When prompting, this means being open to unexpected suggestions and using them as a springboard for refinement. For example, you might ask the AI to generate ideas for a blog post, and while the initial suggestions may not be perfect, they might inspire a direction you hadn't considered. Collaboration requires trust, and when you allow AI to contribute creatively, it often enhances your own work.

The third shift, from perfection to catalyst, reframes how we see AI's role. Many people approach AI with the expectation that it will deliver flawless results. This is a recipe for frustration. Instead, view generative AI as a catalyst for creativity and collaboration. It's not about delivering perfect outputs but sparking ideas, refining concepts, and enabling rapid iteration. For example, if you're drafting a campaign email, the AI's first draft might need significant editing. But instead of seeing this as a failure, recognize it as a starting point, one that accelerates your creative process. AI thrives as a collaborative partner; tell it what you need it to change.

The fourth shift, from mastery to lifelong learning, emphasizes adaptability. Many approach generative AI with the goal of mastering it entirely, as if it's a static tool with fixed rules. The reality is that AI is continuously evolving. Its capabilities—and our understanding of them—will grow over time. This mindset invites you to see every interaction as an opportunity to learn. Each prompt you refine, every insight you gain, builds your AI toolkit.

Finally, the shift from efficiency to enhancement expands how we think about AI's value. While generative AI is undeniably a powerful tool for saving time, its true potential lies in enhancing quality and impact. It's not just about doing things faster. It's about doing them better. When crafting prompts, this means using AI not merely to automate repetitive tasks but to elevate your work. For instance, you can use AI to add depth to your copywriting, explore diverse perspectives, or experiment with formats you might not have considered. By viewing AI as a means of enhancement, you unlock its ability to amplify your creativity and elevate outcomes beyond what you could achieve alone.

These mindset shifts redefine how we approach prompting, making it a dynamic, creative process rather than a rigid task. When you embrace these shifts, you move from simply using AI to partnering with it, and that's where the real power lies. If you or your team would like to attend our Generative AI Masterclass so you can use AI effectively, scan the QR code. The better you understand how to collaborate with new technology, the more powerful your results will be.

TAKE ACTION

As a leader, you have the ability to engage with new technologies and opportunities, and it starts with asking the right questions and taking intentional steps to understand their potential. The following exercises and reflection points are designed to help you apply the ideas from this chapter to your unique context. Take time to work through them, either on your own or with your team, and use them as a springboard for meaningful conversations and actionable insights.

Reflective Questions

- Think about a time when your institution had to adapt to a major change. What worked well in that process? What could have been done differently?
- What assumptions do you currently hold about generative AI or other emerging technologies? Are those assumptions based on experience, fear, or secondhand information?
- What new technologies has your institution adopted recently? How were those decisions made, and what was the outcome?
- How comfortable are you with using AI tools? What specific steps can you take to increase your comfort and proficiency?
- Consider a technology you've dismissed or delegated in the past. What questions could you ask to better understand its potential?

Action Steps

- Pick one AI tool, like ChatGPT, and spend 15–30 minutes exploring its capabilities. Try using it for brainstorming, drafting content, or generating ideas. Better yet, if you have never used it, ask for meal plans, help with your golf game, or other personal engagement. Reflect on what worked and where you saw limitations.
- Have a conversation with your team about their perceptions of generative AI or another emerging technology. What concerns do they have? What opportunities do they see?
- Reach out to a colleague or peer at another institution who is actively using AI or a similar technology. Ask about their experiences, challenges, and advice for getting started.
- Research one new technology relevant to your institution—whether it's AI, electric vehicles, or something else. Look for insights from multiple sources, including experts, critics, and neutral observers.
- Imagine it's five years from now, and AI has become as ubiquitous as electricity. What role does it play in your institution? How has it changed the way you lead, teach, and operate? What steps could you take today to prepare for that future?

4

MARKETING FOR GENERATIONS: 👍 = PASSIVE AGGRESSIVE

"Pop culture is the politics of the 21st century."
—John Kenneth Muir

THE DIVIDE BETWEEN GENERATIONS often shows up in the most unexpected places—like a single emoji. For example, when Gen Z employees update their Millennial manager on a project through Slack, the manager might respond with a " 👍 " to let them know they understand and approve. But instead of feeling reassured, the Gen Z employee feels irritated and unsure. To them, the thumbs-up emoji doesn't signify agreement or acknowledgment. It feels passive aggressive, like their manager didn't really care to take the time to respond to the update. Or worse yet, that there is a message of disapproval or irritation. They wonder why their manager couldn't just say 'got it' or 'sounds good'?

This reaction stems from how Gen Z approaches communication. Unlike older generations who might see the emoji as a practical way to convey agreement, Gen Z, who largely prefer texting over phone calls, interpret it as cold or insincere. That said, they surprisingly offer some leniency to older generations, such as Gen X and Boomer, recognizing that emoji nuances often escape them.

What's fascinating is how Gen Z has developed an entire subculture around emojis,[28] transforming them into symbols of deeper, often unspoken meanings. This generational phenomenon echoes what used to be limited to high school cliques filled with slang, acronyms, and insider knowledge that adults couldn't decipher. But today, these divides have become more pervasive, thanks to platforms like Instagram and TikTok, where each generation builds its unique digital lexicon.

The growing divide between generations, even over something as small as emoji use, shows just how different our worldviews have become. Emojis used to feel universal. Everyone was on the same page. Now, they're more like a reflection of the gaps between us, shaping how we connect, communicate, and make sense of each other.

I was listening to Malcolm Gladwell's *Revenge of the Tipping Point*,[29] and he shared a fascinating example of how culture can shift the way we understand the world. He explained that back in the 1980s, there were just three major television networks, and everyone watched the same shows. Cultural moments were shared experiences. One example he highlighted was the word "Holocaust." Before 1978, the term wasn't widely used to describe the atrocities of World War II. That changed when NBC aired a mini-series titled *Holocaust*. The series brought the term into the mainstream, and if you look at the data, its usage skyrocketed afterward. It became a defining word for the historic tragedy, all because of one piece of popular media.

Popular culture has the power to shape history and define how we think and talk about the world. It's easy to dismiss these generational quirks as superficial, but they point to shifting worldviews shaped by the cultural moments that define each era. One of the best illustrations of this comes from *Back to the Future*. When Marty McFly travels back to 1955 and tries to convince Doc Brown he's from 1985, the conversation goes like this:[30]

Doc Brown: "Then tell me, future boy, who's President of the United States in 1985?"

Marty: "Ronald Reagan."

Doc Brown: "Ronald Reagan? The actor?" *[Rolls his eyes.]* "Ha! Then who's Vice President, Jerry Lewis? I suppose Jane Wyman is the First Lady! And Jack Benny is Secretary of the Treasury!"

Later, while examining Marty's video camera, Doc adds: "No wonder your president has to be an actor. He's gotta look good on television."

The humor lands because it highlights the cultural gap between two generations. What seems perfectly normal to one group can feel absurd to another, until the culture shifts. That line about Reagan being an actor turned president captures the moment television became an influence instead of just enter-tainment. In the same way, emojis, memes, and digital shorthand have become the new cultural language for younger generations.

These generational shifts are windows into how each gener-ation prefers to connect. From the shorthand texts of Gen Z to the carefully crafted emails of Millennials and the phone calls cherished by Boomers, these habits reveal how each generation relates to the world and each other. As marketers, who want to reach our mission-fit students, we need to meet them where they are and speak their language, on their terms.

THE GENERATIONAL EDGE

At many institutions, the topic of generational diversity tends to get reduced to surface-level stereotypes. Boomers resist change, Gen Z can't handle criticism, and Millennials need too much validation. But what if these assumptions are costing you inno-vation, collaboration, and institutional resilience?

That's the premise behind *Gentelligence*, a movement and methodology created by Megan Gerhardt, PhD, professor of management and leadership at Miami University. In her book Gentelligence: *The Revolutionary Approach to Leading an Intergenerational Workforce*,[31] Gerhardt argues that generational diversity is a form of diversity that most leaders overlook and most organizations mismanage.

Her research challenges leaders to move beyond passive acceptance of generational differences and start using them as strategic assets. As she puts it, "We challenge leaders to go beyond simply accepting generational differences to leverage them proactively to increase engagement, innovation, and organizational success." In a higher education context, this might look like inviting younger staff to lead initiatives around digital engagement or social media strategy, areas where they often have native fluency, while tapping into the institutional memory and crisis-tested wisdom of more experienced colleagues when navigating budget constraints or accreditation reviews.

Gerhardt isn't suggesting you coddle younger employees or dismiss older ones. What she's advocating for is a more nuanced and intentional approach, one that views generational differences as tools to unlock greater collaboration, not as problems to manage. That could mean designing cross-generational mentoring programs, updating faculty onboarding to address digital literacy gaps, or creating space in cabinet meetings to hear a broader range of perspectives, from recent hires to senior administrators. In other words, it's not about leveling everyone to the same style, it's about leveraging the full range of generational strengths to serve your institution's mission more effectively.

Through her Gentelligence framework, she outlines four key practices that can help leaders do just that:

- **Identify Assumptions:** Challenge your knee-jerk reactions about generational behavior. Instead of assuming someone's age dictates their attitude, get curious about what's really driving it.
- **Adjust the Lens:** Recognize that every generation was shaped by a different world. Context matters. What seems odd or inefficient to you might feel like common sense to someone from a different era.

- **Build Trust:** Create a space where people of all ages feel seen, heard, and respected. Without psychological safety, intergenerational collaboration breaks down before it starts.
- **Expand the Pie:** Instead of making generational diversity a zero-sum game, look for win-win opportunities. Foster environments where older workers can learn from younger ones and vice versa.

I believe Gerhardt's work is especially relevant in higher education, where generational divides show up everywhere—from how faculty approach technology in the classroom, to how staff communicate across departments, to how marketing teams craft messages for prospective students and their parents. You'll find Gen Z staff advocating for Slack while senior administrators still prefer email, or seasoned faculty pushing back on changes to curriculum delivery formats that younger colleagues champion. And as institutions face increasingly complex challenges, from enrollment cliffs to shifting student expectations, the ability to draw on the unique strengths of each generation is non-negotiable.

Her message is clear, ignoring generational dynamics won't make them go away. But by becoming students of those dynamics, leaders can turn a source of friction into a powerful competitive edge.

FROM CASSETTES TO TIKTOK

Every generation's way of communicating is shaped by the technology, culture, and trends of their time. A perfect example of this surfaced on TikTok, where a Gen Z creator stumbled upon a cassette tape and hilariously tried to piece together its purpose and history. She referenced it as being from the "late 1900s," assumed it was single use, and even speculated that Tom Cruise must've been in a band because of his face on the tape's case (in reality, the tape was the soundtrack of Tom Cruise's 1988 movie "Cocktail"). She then proceeds on a prolonged chain-of-thought connection of the Beach Boys' song *"Kokomo"* to the Olsen twins from *Full House* through Marvel's *Scarlet Witch* as a way to explain her discovery to her audience. You can watch her full video by scanning the QR code.[32]

This video made me laugh, but it also made me think. Her attempt to connect the dots is a perfect example of "backward thinking," or trying to understand something from another era without enough context or research. And that's exactly what happens when we make assumptions about how to market to a generation without fully understanding them. If we base our messaging on our own worldviews instead of theirs, it's no different than her assuming Tom Cruise was in a band because she lacked context about the movie he starred in.

Marketing across generations is about understanding and including multiple perspectives in the process. In higher education, for instance, our messaging isn't aimed at a single audience. We're speaking to students of all ages, parents, influencers, and sometimes even grandparents, each with their own generational lens.

This is why it's so important to include different generations as collaborators in the creative process. In my previous book, *Chasing Mission Fit*, we discussed the importance of asking students what they think rather than relying solely on the input of boards or administrators. I'll add that we need to extend this approach even further. While students are a critical audience, they aren't the only ones affected by our messaging. Parents, alumni, staff, and even prospective donors—each representing different generations—bring their own perspectives and expectations to the table. By involving these groups early in the creative process, we gain insights that help us craft messages which resonate across the spectrum, not just within a single silo.

Gary Vaynerchuk's excellent book *Daytrading Attention*[33] highlights this shift in how brands approach research and creative development. He advocates that instead of relying on traditional, top-down research processes, we should be using social media as a testing ground. Post organically, experiment with different messaging styles, and see what resonates. Use that real-time feedback to refine your content before transitioning it to paid campaigns or broader media.

This strategy also applies to generational understanding. Content that resonates with Gen Z on TikTok might fall flat with Millennials on Instagram or parents on Facebook. Testing your messaging with each audience allows you to uncover what works best for their preferences.

For example, while the Silent Generation may prefer direct mail and newspapers, Millennials largely dismiss these as outdated and irrelevant. However, Gen Z finds newspapers fascinating because of their novelty and nostalgia. You can't assume you know what will work for a given generation. You have to engage, experiment, and listen if you want your message to land.

GENERATIONS EVOLVE, AND SO SHOULD YOUR MESSAGING

If you want to understand how generations think, look at how they've adapted to the tools and technology of their era. Take music as an example. When I was a kid, my mom had an 8-track player and vinyl records (some that I remember were Elton John's *Greatest Hits* on vinyl LP and the 8-Track of REO Speedwagon's *Hi Infidelity*). My favorite song that I purchased was Rick Springfield's *Jessie's Girl*, and I would listen to it on a forty-five vinyl in my room, feeling like the coolest kid ever. Then, when I turned twelve, I got a stereo with dual cassette decks—what game changer! I could record songs off the radio and replay them over and over or purchase the album on cassette.

Fast forward to college, and CDs became the big thing. Suddenly, I had to buy Rick Springfield's entire *Working Class Dog* CD to listen to *Jessie's Girl* again, this time on disc. And then came the late '90s, when MP3 players started showing up. I even worked as a designer on the packaging for one of the first models for RCA (Radio Corporation of America), which used to be *the* consumer electronics company before Apple took over.[34] It could hold a whopping twenty songs, and if I wanted *Jessie's Girl* on it, I had to either rip it from my CD or go the illegal route and download it off of Napster.

Then came the iPod and iTunes, and guess what? I had to buy the song again, from Apple this time. Finally, Spotify arrived, and everything changed. Now, I don't need to "own" *Jessie's Girl* at all. I can stream it anywhere, anytime, straight from my phone.

Think about that evolution. I've purchased six or seven formats just to listen to the same song, and every time, it was because that new format made things easier or more convenient. Each change wasn't about the song itself. It was about the benefit that new technology provided.

That's how generations adapt. They chase the benefits that make their lives easier or better, and their behaviors shift as technology evolves. For Gen Z, that's why texting is king. It's quick, easy, and gets the point across. Need something more personal? They'll FaceTime. But call them out of the blue? Good luck. They might not even answer unless you text first to ask for permission.

To older generations, this might seem strange. My friend and I were laughing recently because he thought it was so odd to send a text before calling. "Why not just call?" he said. But what feels natural for one generation doesn't feel natural for another. It's just another example of how technology and culture shape the way we connect.

As higher ed marketers, we can't afford to assume that what worked yesterday will work tomorrow. Generational preferences aren't set in stone; they continually shift as new tools and opportunities emerge.

How do we keep up? By staying curious. Instead of locking into one way of communicating, we need to ask questions and actively listen. Ask yourself what benefits your audience is chasing. How can you position your message as the shortcut to those benefits? How can you stay flexible enough to adapt as their preferences evolve?

Generations evolve, and your messaging should too. If you can meet them where they are *and* where they're going, you'll have a much better chance of connecting in a meaningful way.

WHERE ATTENTION GOES NEXT

Here's where I'm going to put on my prediction hat. It's no secret that social media has been a dominant force in how we connect and communicate over the past two decades. But what if the next generation decides it's time to leave it behind? There's already evidence suggesting they might.

Another aspect of Gary Vee's book *Daytrading Attention* that caught my attention was when he talked about finding where people's focus is now, and more importantly, where it's heading. He predicts that in 10 to 15 years, social media as we know it today will be a thing of the past. The next big platforms? Likely VR (virtual reality) and AR (augmented reality). And no, not the clunky headsets we think of now. Imagine lightweight glasses replacing phones entirely, letting us talk, browse, and experience immersive digital spaces seamlessly.

I believe the first generations to leave social media behind might be the ones who grew up with it (Gen Z and Gen Alpha) largely because of growing health concerns. Just like how younger generations were the first to reject smoking or embrace seatbelts, they're now the first to push back against the negative impacts of social media. Depression, loneliness, and "doom scrolling" have taken their toll. Many in these generations are starting to say, "no thanks" and deleting social media off their phone entirely.

We might look back in a few decades and wonder why we ever thought scrolling through feeds all day was a good idea. It could be the equivalent of reviewing the old advertisements where doctors recommended cigarettes.[35] [36] And just like smoking, the shift away from it will be because the younger generation wants new ways to connect, ways that prioritize mental health and meaningful interaction.

That doesn't mean they'll abandon digital communication entirely. But younger generations are increasingly opting for more intentional and personal forms of communication. As higher ed marketers, we need to watch these shifts closely. Where are they going? What tools and platforms will they use to connect next?

The tools we rely on today won't always be there, and that's okay. The key is to stay adaptable and curious while keeping our finger on the pulse of where the next wave of communication is headed. Instead of clinging to old strategies, we have to be students of these generational changes, following the crowd as their watering holes[37] shift so we can continue to connect with our audiences.

TAKE ACTION

Understanding generational differences and communication preferences is a practical skill that can transform the way you connect with students, parents, and other key audiences. The following exercises and reflection points are designed to help you apply the ideas from this chapter to your unique context. Take time to work through them, either on your own or with your team, and use them as a springboard for meaningful conversations and actionable insights.

Reflective Questions

- Think about the primary and secondary audiences your institution serves. How do their generational differences shape the way they expect to be communicated with?
- Reflect on the platforms your institution currently uses for marketing. Are they aligned with where each generation spends their time and attention?
- How has your institution adapted to generational changes in the past? What lessons can you apply to future shifts?
- Consider a marketing campaign your institution has run recently. Was it designed with multiple generations in mind, or did it lean toward one specific audience?
- How often do you test your messaging with different generational audiences? What insights have you gained, and where could you improve?

- What assumptions do you or your team hold about specific generations? How can you challenge those assumptions to better understand their needs and preferences?

Action Steps

- Identify three key generational groups your institution serves (e.g., Gen Z students, Millennial adult students, Gen X parents and grandparents, Boomer alumni). Research their preferred communication styles and platforms.
- Use social media as a sandbox for testing. Post content aimed at different generational groups (or decades) and analyze engagement metrics. What resonates, and why?
- Try creating a campaign or message tailored to a generation you don't typically focus on. Test it with a small audience and gather feedback.
- Assemble a diverse focus group representing different generations at your institution—students, parents, alumni, staff—and ask for their feedback on current messaging.
- The next time you plan a marketing campaign, involve representatives from multiple generations in the brainstorming phase. Include the generational perspectives they bring to the table and test the effectiveness of the campaign.

5

MARKETING PROGRAMS: HOW DO I SELL SOMETHING NOBODY WANTS TO BUY?

"Don't find customers for your products, find products for your customers."
—Seth Godin

EVERY YEAR, millions of people flock to Disney parks, knowing full well they'll be standing in long lines, paying premium prices, and leaving utterly exhausted. And yet, they keep coming back. Why? Because Disney has mastered the art of creating experiences. From the moment visitors walk through the gates, they're transported into meticulously crafted worlds where every detail, including the music playing in the background, to the scents wafting from the bakeries on Main Street, are designed to evoke wonder.

People step into stories. They soar over Neverland with Peter Pan or join a swashbuckling adventure with Jack Sparrow. Every turn presents a new moment of magic. Between the parade, the fireworks, or encounters with their favorite character, it shows them what it feels like to be a kid again. Even the simple joys, like collecting pins, create emotional connections that keep people coming back.

This kind of seamless, immersive experience doesn't happen by accident. The business side of Disney carefully designs, packages, and markets these experiences to meet the desires of their audience. Every interaction exists because Disney understands what people want and delivers it in a way that feels effortless.

Higher education should take notes. Too many institutions hesitate to see themselves as businesses. They resist the idea that their programs are products, fearing that marketing them as such diminishes their value. But people are buying these programs. They are investing years of their life and tens of thousands of dollars with the expectation of a tangible return: a degree, a better career, a more secure future, an experience. If that's not a product, what is?

Yet, many institutions struggle to market their programs because they fail to recognize what they are actually selling. A business knows that to make a sale, you need to understand:

- What is the product?
- Who is it for?
- How do you make it irresistible?

Disney knows selling a plush Mickey Mouse in a gift shop is different from selling a $10,000 family vacation to Disney World.

And because they know this, they market those products differently. Higher education should do the same. Are you selling a degree? A career outcome? Or a transformational life experience? Because if you're still selling "small class sizes" and "a close-knit community," you're missing the mark.[38]

The question isn't just how do we enroll more students, it's how do we make this experience so compelling that students feel they can't afford to miss it? If you can answer that, you'll stop pursuing students and start attracting the ones who truly belong at your institution.

THE MARKETPLACE REALITY

Higher education isn't the only industry that faces the challenge of declining demand. Every business, from retail to entertainment, understands that demand drives survival.

Look at Nike. Nike knows that Air Jordans sell. But they don't just put out one version of the shoe and call it a day. They've expanded the Air Jordan into an entire product line, with variations, limited releases, and collaborations. When they realized sneakers tied to high-profile athletes sell more, they expanded their strategy. Now, if there's a sport, there's a Nike-sponsored athlete with a shoe line to match.

Nike also knows when to pivot. Not every collaboration works forever. Take Tiger Woods, for example. For years, Tiger was one of Nike's top athletes, and his partnership with the brand was a massive success. But when his personal life took a hit, and demand for his branded products declined, Nike made the business decision to step away from the relationship.

This is what smart businesses do. They follow demand. When a product is selling, they invest more. When the market shifts, they pivot. And when demand dies, they retire the product and move on.

Yet in higher education, too many institutions refuse to do this. They cling to programs that no longer attract students. They ignore market signals. They hold onto offerings simply because they've always been there, even when enrollment numbers tell a different story.

When demand for a product disappears, companies don't ask, "How do we sell more of this?" They ask, "What should we be selling instead?" Higher ed leaders need to do the same. If students aren't enrolling in a program, that's not a marketing problem—it's a product problem. The solution isn't to push harder; it's to step back, reassess, and make sure what you're offering is actually wanted.

THE ACADEMY VS. THE MARKETPLACE

I once worked with an institution on a website redesign, and as part of the process, I met with the leadership team, including deans from different colleges. I asked, "What are the top five to ten programs students come here for?"

This might seem like a basic question, but it's one even seasoned institutions often overlook. We can't just look at what you're known for academically. We also need to identify which programs consistently attract mission-fit students, generate inquiries, and convert prospects. Without clarity here, it's impossible to align your messaging, prioritize investments, or build a marketing strategy that plays to your competitive advantage.

But as soon as I asked this question, I could feel the tension in the room. One of the deans—who happened to oversee the history department—got visibly upset and let me know it. He assumed I was saying history wasn't important. That I was suggesting we shouldn't promote it on the homepage, while business or healthcare got all the attention.

That wasn't my point at all. I wasn't making a value judgment. I was making a market judgment. Every program at an institution has worth. But not every program has the same level of demand. If your goal is to attract more students and impact the bottom line, you can't market everything equally.

Now, as many of you reading this book will understand, there is an unspoken divide in higher education between faculty and administration that's been around for centuries. If you've worked in academia, you've seen it firsthand. On one side, you have the academy, including the faculty, the scholars, and the keepers of knowledge. Their traditions date back to the Middle Ages when universities were first founded as places of intellectual pursuit and scholars gathered to debate. On the other side, you have the business of higher education, including the leadership teams responsible for making sure the institution functions in the real world. The problem is that the academy side and the business side don't always see eye to eye.

Many faculty members believe their job is to impart knowledge, to expand human understanding, and to teach what they deem essential, not necessarily what the market demands. That's a noble mission. But when it comes to designing new programs, this mindset can become a liability. No matter how intellectually valuable a program might be, if students don't see its value in the job market, they won't pay for it.

That's where things get tricky. I've seen this play out countless times. A passionate department designs a new program that they believe is groundbreaking, something they think students *need* to learn. They put together the curriculum, map out the courses, and propose it to the administration. But when it launches, no one signs up.

It's frustrating for everyone. The faculty believe in the program. The institution has invested in it. But without student demand, it becomes a financial drain rather than a strategic advantage.

This happens because the academy often operates outside of business needs. Faculty are experts in their disciplines, whether that's history, philosophy, literature, or STEM. Their job is to push the boundaries of their fields. But most faculty don't have experience in marketing. They're not trained to analyze market demand, identify student interest, or position a program to attract applicants. That disconnect can lead to programs that, while academically valuable, simply don't have an audience willing to buy them.

MARKETING WITH STRATEGY, NOT EMOTION

To effectively market a program, you need to answer three key questions:

1. **Is there a market for it?** Are students actively searching for this type of program or your particular version of it? Is there demand in the workforce? Are students asking for it?

2. **Do you have the capacity to deliver it?** If students enroll, do you have the faculty, facilities, and infrastructure to support them?

3. **Does it make financial sense?** Some programs are inherently more expensive to run. A history degree, for example, might require only classroom space and professors. A nursing program, on the other hand, involves expensive equipment, clinical partnerships, and highly specialized faculty. That higher overhead must be factored into how you position and price the program.

These are the realities that institutions must consider if they want to grow enrollment and stay financially sustainable. That doesn't mean history, philosophy, or other lower-enrollment programs don't matter. It means they need different strategies. They might rely more on storytelling, alumni success stories, or cross-promotion with other disciplines. But the homepage? The first thing prospective students see? That space should be reserved for your institution's most in-demand, high-enrollment programs.

If institutions want to sell something that people do want to buy, they need to:

- Acknowledge the reality of market demand,
- Prioritize their most sought-after programs in marketing efforts, and
- Make data-driven decisions instead of emotional ones.

When faculty and administration understand this distinction, institutions can bridge the gap between academic tradition and marketplace reality, ensuring the longevity of the institution and the success of its students.

NAVIGATING THE FACULTY-ADMINISTRATION DIVIDE

How do you combat this disconnect between the academic side and the business side? Carefully.

Higher education is full of delicate balances, and few are more complex than the relationship between faculty and administration. If you charge in headfirst with a "business-first" mindset, you risk alienating faculty who see themselves as stewards of knowledge rather than market-driven professionals. But if you tiptoe around the issue and avoid hard conversations, you risk programs that continue to drain resources without bringing in students.

One of the keys to navigating this divide is recognizing that most leaders fall somewhere along a spectrum. On one end, you have those who lean heavily into academic tradition, they are leaders who prioritize faculty governance, intellectual rigor, and the preservation of institutional identity. On the other hand, you have those with more of a business orientation, leaders focused on enrollment growth, financial health, and market positioning.

Most presidents, provosts, and senior leaders aren't firmly in one camp or the other. They're constantly balancing these competing priorities, working to honor the academic mission while keeping the institution sustainable. Understanding where your leadership falls on this spectrum can help you frame ideas more effectively and find common ground for collaboration.

Let's look at each side of this spectrum.

The Business-Minded President

When a president is business-minded, they bring a fresh perspective that academia sometimes lacks. They look at student recruitment like customer acquisition. They want ROI on marketing efforts. They focus on making programs competitive and marketable.

This approach can be incredibly effective. But sometimes, a business-minded leader can be like a bull in a China shop, charging in with changes that disrupt the culture of the institution. Faculty, already wary of administrative interference, may dig in their heels even further. If the president doesn't take the time to understand academic culture, they risk losing the very people they need to execute their vision.

How to work with a business-first leader:

- Frame things in terms of measurable impact. They want numbers, so bring them data on program demand, student interest, and enrollment trends.
- Help bridge the gap with faculty. They may not have the patience (or the political finesse) to manage faculty relationships, but you can be the person who translates between the two worlds.
- Encourage them to pace their changes. Higher ed moves slower than corporate America, and if they try to overhaul everything at once, they'll meet resistance.

The Academician President

When a president leans toward the academic side of the spectrum, they often bring a deep respect for intellectual tradition and academic freedom. They understand faculty culture from the inside, having spent years in the classroom or the lab, and they tend to lead with collaboration, consensus, and a commitment to preserving the institution's educational mission. These presidents are typically thoughtful, principled decision-makers who work hard to honor the values of the academy.

That same thoughtful approach, however, can sometimes slow down action. In an effort to be inclusive and thorough, decisions may pass through multiple committees and rounds of review. Business language may feel uncomfortable or even inappropriate, especially if it seems to reduce education to a commodity. But while these leaders are doing their due diligence, the external environment doesn't pause. Market conditions shift, enrollment trends evolve, and competitor institutions may move faster.

How to work with an academic-first leader:

- Emphasize the urgency of market realities. They may not naturally think in business terms, but they understand survival. Show them how quickly the landscape is changing and how inaction can hurt the institution.
- Present data in a way that aligns with their values. Instead of talking about "market share" or "ROI," frame it as student success, institutional sustainability, and program viability.
- Help them avoid analysis paralysis. Some decisions require careful thought. Others require action now. Be the person who helps them distinguish between the two.

Finding the Balance

Ultimately, the most effective institutions and leaders find a balance between business strategy and academic tradition. If you lean *too far* into the business mindset, you risk turning education into something that's only valued in dollars and job placements. If you lean *too far* into the academic mindset, you risk becoming out of touch with student needs and disconnected from the job market.

Many campus leaders are in a unique position to bridge this divide. You understand your institution's mission, and you're attuned to the pressures of enrollment, budget, and competition. You interact with students, faculty, staff, and stakeholders across generations and disciplines. That gives you a rare vantage point, one that allows you to act as a translator between academic values and market realities.

When you can help both sides see the bigger picture, you create space for alignment, collaboration, and meaningful progress. The challenge isn't just enrolling more students. Sometimes, it's helping your institution see the world as it really is, so it can adapt, evolve, and thrive.

THE REAL WAY TO SELL SOMETHING NOBODY WANTS TO BUY

You don't. No, really. If nobody wants to buy the program, you shouldn't be selling it. However, you need to prove whether somebody does, or doesn't, want what's for sale. Before launching a new program, the first question should always be: Why are we doing this?

In *Start With Why*, Simon Sinek explains that truly successful organizations don't just focus on what they do or how they do it. They start with why they exist in the first place. He writes, "People don't buy what you do; they buy why you do it."[39]

If a program is being proposed because there's a need for it in the workforce, because employers are asking for graduates with these skills, and because students see it as a pathway to their desired future, then the *why* is clear. But if the program exists solely because an administrator or board member thinks it would "round out" the institution's offerings, it's not grounded in real demand.

Market research plays a key role in uncovering demand, and there are two ways to approach it: formalized research and ad hoc research.

Formalized research means hiring a third party to conduct surveys or interviews with potential students to gauge interest in a program. Think about how much polling happens during a presidential election. Candidates typically don't just assume what their constituents want. They gather data. Institutions should do the same. Find out how much capacity your region has for another MBA program. Measure how much brand awareness your institution has compared to competitors. Conduct structured interviews with prospective students and ask standardized questions like rating their interest on a scale from one to ten or responding to true/false statements about program appeal. If you need precise results, you might want to bring in a statistician to help ensure you have a reliable sample size.

AI tools can make this process easier. If you describe the program you want to launch and the kind of data you need, AI can generate targeted survey questions. It can even help refine your outreach strategy by identifying key trends in student decision-making based on the information you gathered.

For institutions without the budget for formal research, ad hoc research can be a valuable option. Free tools like SurveyMonkey allow institutions to send out simple surveys asking potential students how likely they would be to take a specific class or pursue a particular degree. But this kind of research only works if it's directed at the *right* people. You have to send it to the individuals who would actually consider enrolling, not to faculty members, administrators, or internal committees. You need to stick to your watering holes and your ideal mission-fit students.[40]

Asking the right people the right questions is the only way to know whether a program is viable. It's not enough to ask what students want. You also need to ask how they want it delivered. Would they prefer an in-person experience? A hybrid model? A fully online program? Do they even know your institution offers this kind of program? The answers will shape not just whether the program should exist, but how it should be marketed.

Jeremy Taylor, Vice President of Enrollment Management at Defiance College, understood this. After hearing me speak about AI and mission-fit students, he took a closer look at his institution's data. Historically, Defiance College had focused its recruitment efforts on the seven rural counties surrounding the institution. It's what they had always done, and for years it worked…until it didn't.[41]

Rather than doubling down on the same shrinking pool of students, Jeremy decided to expand his search. Instead of just focusing on the rural Northwest Ohio counties around the institution, he started recruiting in Cleveland, Cincinnati, Detroit, and Chicago, places where there were far more students who might need what Defiance had to offer but had never even heard of the institution.

The result? A 78% increase in enrollment. And he had no prior background in enrollment or admissions.

KNOW WHEN TO SUNSET

Sunsetting a program is one of the toughest decisions in higher education. If only one student is enrolling, it's a clear sign the market has likely moved on. A program that thrived in the 1970s may no longer serve today's students. Especially if the career path looks different than it did fifty years ago. When the market shifts, institutions need to be willing to shift with it.

The problem is, sunsetting a program isn't just eliminating a line item on a course catalog. It often means reassigning faculty, reskilling instructors, or in some cases, making difficult layoffs. These decisions carry emotional and political weight, making them easy to postpone and difficult to navigate. But ignoring the problem doesn't make it go away, and hoping a program will magically become relevant again isn't a strategy, it's denial.

This book is about knowing the right questions to ask, having the courage to ask them, and being prepared to act on the answers. It's easy to placate people in institutions that are resistant to change, especially when those changes directly impact faculty. Every institution has different internal politics, and in some, the faculty has more decision-making power than others. But no matter the governance structure, one principle should always apply: the tail shouldn't wag the dog.

Too often, I've seen presidents recognize that a program is no longer viable, only to be voted out the door because faculty members refuse to let it go. The result is an institution stuck with an unmarketable program that drains resources while enrollment numbers continue to decline.

This is where the art of politics comes in. In *How to Win Friends and Influence People*,[42] Dale Carnegie emphasizes that before you can get people to accept tough decisions, you must earn their trust. Once trust is established, you create a culture where asking tough questions isn't seen as a threat but becomes part of the institution's normal decision-making process. When you demonstrate the ability to improve efficiencies in other areas first, you build the credibility needed for harder decisions. So, when it's time to sunset a program, stakeholders are more likely to trust that it's a thoughtful, well-considered move, not a knee-jerk reaction.

There are several key questions every institution should ask when evaluating whether to sunset a program:

- **If this is a new program, where did the idea come from?** What market research supports it?
- **Is there actual market demand?** Has it been tested? Often, faculty members develop a program based on personal interest or a grant opportunity, rather than market need. Sometimes, a grant covers the first year of a program, but after that funding runs out, the institution is left with a program that has no real market. If a business were launching a new product, they wouldn't invest $100,000 in production molds before determining whether there's a customer base. Yet in higher education, this happens all the time. It's the classic *"If we build it, they will come"* mindset. But the truth is, nobody

is whispering from a cornfield like in *Field of Dreams*.[43] You have to go out and do the work.

- **What does our historical data tell us?** If enrollment has been declining for years, what's the reason? Are students choosing alternative programs at your own institution? Have they turned to online competitors?

- **What does competitive data tell us?** If other institutions of similar size have cut the program, that's a sign. If those same institutions are seeing success with the program, the issue may not be the program itself but how it's being marketed.

- **Are we keeping this program just because we're the "only game in town"?** Being the only institution in the area offering a certain degree isn't a justification for keeping it. If no one in town wants the program, it doesn't matter if there's no competition.

I once worked with a small Bible college that was struggling with enrollment. They kept telling me, "We're the best-kept secret in town. If more people just knew about our Bible program, we'd be packed." But I had to push back and ask the tough question: how many people in your town want a Bible degree?

Even if 30% of the population attends church regularly, how many of those individuals are interested in pursuing formal theological education? Some are children. Some are retired. Many are already established in their careers and aren't looking to change paths. Once you narrow it down to the people who are both *interested* in a Bible degree and *at the right stage of life to pursue it,* the number shrinks dramatically. The issue wasn't awareness, it was demand.

If an institution is struggling to attract students to a program, it needs to be honest about whether it's targeting the right audience. If the local market isn't large enough to sustain a program, the institution needs to look beyond its immediate surroundings and rethink its approach. That might mean pivoting to an online format, expanding recruitment efforts to a different region, or, in some cases, making the tough decision to sunset the program altogether.

Sometimes, the challenge isn't that a program isn't marketable, it's that the market you've always relied on is no longer big enough to sustain it. Institutions that have historically served rural populations may need to look to urban areas. Or institutions that have traditionally catered to one demographic may need to broaden their outreach strategies.

Remember, all of this brings us back to the existing enrollment cliff. The next generation of students is going to be more diverse, and their needs and expectations will be different from those of previous generations. Institutions that fail to recognize this shift and rely on outdated recruitment models will struggle. The institutions that thrive will be the ones willing to find the right students and meet them where they are.

TAKE ACTION

By taking a proactive approach to evaluating programs, targeting mission-fit students, and making data-driven decisions, your institution can avoid the trap of trying to sell something nobody wants to buy. The following exercises and reflection points are designed to help you apply the ideas from this chapter to your unique context. Take time to work through them, either on your own or with your team, and use them as a springboard for meaningful conversations and actionable insights.

Reflective Questions

- How does your institution currently determine whether a program has real market demand? Is your process based on internal preferences, or do you rely on external data and research?
- Think about a program that has struggled with enrollment in recent years. Has the institution conducted any formal or informal market research to determine whether there is still demand for it?
- Are there programs at your institution that have seen declining enrollment for multiple years? What conversations, if any, have taken place about whether they should be continued?
- Does your institution have a clear process for evaluating when a program should be restructured, repositioned, or sunsetted? If not, how can you start building one?

- If a program isn't attracting students, is the issue market demand, or is it a marketing problem? How can you determine the difference?
- What data do you have on the students who are most likely to succeed at your institution? How well are you aligning your marketing efforts to attract those mission-fit students?

Action Steps

- Identify three to five programs with the lowest enrollment over the past three years. Gather data on their historical trends, competitive landscape, and student demand.
- If a program is underperforming, brainstorm ways to reposition it. Could it be modernized? Could it be marketed to a different audience? If not, what would need to happen for the institution to consider sunsetting it?
- Choose one program—either existing or proposed—and conduct a market research test. Use surveys, AI-generated deep research,[44] or direct outreach to potential students and employers to gauge demand.
- Start a conversation with leadership about how the institution makes decisions regarding new and existing programs. What role does data currently play, and where is there room for improvement?
- Set a goal to review program performance data on a regular basis—annually, biannually, or quarterly—rather than waiting until a crisis forces action.

6

DIGITAL MARKETING: $1200 ON A KEYWORD!?

"99% of people don't market in the year that we are actually living in."

—Gary Vaynerchuck

I'VE REVIEWED A LOT of higher ed marketing budgets over the years, and if there's one thing I've learned, it's that institutions love to spend money on digital ads, but they don't always know what they are paying for.

One of the first things we at Caylor Solutions do when we audit an institution's marketing efforts is dig into their paid media campaigns. We're looking for anomalies, places where money is leaking out without anyone realizing it. Because when you're bidding on keywords in a PPC (pay-per-click) campaign, the cost isn't fixed. It's an auction. Just like in a live auction, some things are simply worth more. The key phrase "Master of

Business Administration" for example, is an incredibly competitive search term. If you want to show up at the top of Google for that phrase, you should expect to pay at least $200 per click.

So, when I came across an institution that was regularly paying $1,200 per click for a keyword, I nearly fell out of my chair.

Let me put this in perspective. In digital marketing, a "conversion" typically means someone clicks an ad and lands on your webpage. That's it. But a lot of institutions mistakenly assume "conversion" means someone fills out an inquiry form, which is a big mistake when paying for a keyword at that cost.

In higher education, the industry average for a landing page conversion rate (i.e., someone filling out a form after clicking an ad) is between 5-10%—that means even if your ad is performing well, only one out of every twenty people will take action. So, if you're spending $1,200 per click and only one out of twenty fills out the form, you've just spent $24,000 to get a single lead. And that's just the top of the funnel!

Now let's keep going. Let's say your institution has an average yield rate, and 30% of your leads move from inquiry to application (which is very generous with a typical industry rate of 10-30% yield at this point in the funnel).[45] That means to get one application, you needed to generate three inquiries, at a cost of $96,000.

But wait—there's more. The average scenario for yield from application to enrollment is about 33%. So now, to get one student actually sitting in a classroom on day one, you've had to generate three accepted applications, six inquiries, and spend close to $288,000 just in ad spend. And if that student is enrolling in a $3,500 certificate program, you don't need an

MBA to do the math. You are upside down before the first class even starts.

Compare that scenario to a typical ad scenario, where you're paying $5 per click or even the industry standard of $35 per click, your cost to enroll a student—meaning your cost per acquisition (CPA)—should be around $1,200. That's a whole different ballgame than the $24,000-per-lead senior we just walked through.

Yes, you might have a million-dollar budget. But if that budget isn't being used efficiently, you're just burning cash. A big spend that gets students at any cost isn't a success, it's wasteful. Especially when there are many ways to be more efficient with your digital marketing.

Remember, every dollar you put at the top of the funnel snowballs as it moves down. If your cost per click is too high, then your cost per inquiry skyrockets. If your cost per inquiry is out of control, then your cost per application explodes. By the time you get to actual enrolled students, your return on investment is upside down. And if you aren't tracking all of this, you won't even know what's broken.

I work with institutions that get fifty leads a month and feel good about it. But when I ask them how many of those leads turned into enrolled students, they don't know because they aren't tracking the full path of those students. This is because most institutions have major gaps in their data. They're not using UTM codes (unique tracking links) or pixel tracking to see exactly where a student comes from. I recommend using Google Analytics 4 (GA4) which can track attribution—meaning, it can show you how a student moved through the funnel—but it has to be set up properly. And most institutions simply aren't doing that.

When you don't track correctly, you have no idea if your student came through a paid keyword, a stealth application, an organic search, or a phone call. That means you can't optimize your spending. You might assume your PPC campaign is bringing in all your best leads when in reality, the students filling out applications may have found you through an entirely different channel.

The best way to stop wasting money? Start tracking everything and know what you're paying for. Every keyword, every click, every inquiry. Understand how much it takes from start to finish to get *one* student in a seat. When you understand where your money is going and how your leads are moving through the funnel, you can stop wasting budget on dead-end clicks and start investing in strategies that actually bring in students. That all starts with knowing how digital advertising really works.

WHAT IS DIGITAL ADVERTISING ANYWAYS?

Digital advertising, also known as pay-per-click (PPC) advertising,[46] has become a golden opportunity for marketers. In the early 2000s, Google realized they could monetize their search engine by auctioning off premium ad placements to the highest bidder. At the time, nobody was really doing it. You could buy a keyword for a penny, maybe five cents, and the return on investment was incredible. For institutions and businesses that understood the potential, it was an easy, low-cost way to get in front of the right audience at the exact moment they were searching.

Then, social media entered the picture. Facebook took PPC advertising to another level, allowing advertisers to target users based on their posts, browsing history, and interactions. If someone posted about Pokémon cards, a business selling rare trading cards could serve them an ad instantly. It was a new era of digital intent marketing. But the honeymoon phase didn't last long.

As more organizations jumped into digital advertising, the space became a race to the bottom. Costs skyrocketed as businesses and institutions had to outbid each other just to be seen. Organic reach—what was once free—started to disappear. Facebook, Google, and other platforms realized they could charge for everything. Suddenly, you weren't just bidding for prime real estate on Google; you had to pay just to show up in your followers' news feeds (also known as boosting a post).

Then, as privacy laws tightened, targeting became more difficult. The digital ad market became oversaturated, expensive, and complicated. What started as a simple strategy of purchasing keywords now requires an advanced level of expertise just to see a return on investment.

This is why you need people who really know what they're doing. A solid keyword strategy is critical. But if you hand it off to someone who doesn't understand your industry, they'll likely focus on the wrong keywords which will waste your budget on broad, high-competition searches instead of long-tail keywords[47] that are more specific and cost-effective. We will dive into more examples of long-tail keywords throughout this chapter.

Another problem arose as a huge portion of internet traffic today became bots. In fact, 60% of all internet traffic is automated, and about 60% of PPC ad clicks come from bots. That means a *huge chunk* of your advertising budget is likely going to waste. It's for this reason that we at Caylor Solutions are starting to move away from a heavy reliance on PPC as a core strategy.

I've seen too many institutions pour their entire budget into paid SEM (search engine marketing) thinking it's the only way to attract students. But what happens when that changes?

If Google changes its rules overnight, or if legislation suddenly restricts digital advertising, your entire strategy could disappear in an instant. Just like Thanos snapping his fingers in the classic Marvel *Infinity War* movie, everything shifts, and you are left scrambling. If your entire enrollment strategy is built around digital ads, you're setting yourself up for a crisis when the rules change. And I promise you, one day, they will change.

This is why you can't put all your eggs in the PPC basket. Institutions that truly thrive in digital marketing are the ones that think beyond paid ads. They're not just bidding on keywords, they're building brand awareness, creating demand, and meeting students where they already are. When your entire marketing strategy revolves around PPC, you're gambling on a system that could change at any moment.

Institutions that succeed long-term don't wait for searches to happen. Instead, they build relationships, create engagement, and make their institution impossible to ignore. This means understanding watering holes, the digital and physical spaces where prospective students spend time. By meeting students where they are and leveraging AI-driven insights, institutions can attract the right audience without overpaying for broad, ineffective keywords.

Paid search is a tool, not a strategy. Used wisely, it's valuable. But without a broader marketing plan, it's just an expensive gamble. Next, let's dive into the best practices for PPC advertising in higher education.

Best Practices to Win with PPC

One of the biggest reasons institutions struggle with PPC is that they launch campaigns without a well-defined objective. Too often, institutions focus on general outcomes like "getting more students" or "increasing applications" without specifying how many students they need, how much they're willing to pay for each inquiry, or what success really looks like. Without clear goals, a PPC campaign is just a money drain with no measurable return.

Before running any ads, institutions need to ask themselves, what exactly are we trying to achieve? If the goal is to increase student enrollment, then how many inquiries or applications are needed to make that happen? If the goal is to promote a specific program, how will success be measured? Through clicks, form submissions, or actual enrollments? If the focus is on brand awareness, what are the indicators that the campaign is working? These questions should guide every decision, from keyword selection to ad copy to budget allocation.

Instead of casting a wide net, institutions need to be laser-focused on who they are trying to reach and what those students care about. A prospective student searching for an online MBA while balancing a full-time job has very different priorities than a high school senior looking for an on-campus undergraduate experience. Their motivations, concerns, and even the language they use when searching online will be different. Understanding these nuances is what separates a strong PPC strategy from a wasteful one.

To get this right, institutions need to look at their current enrolled students and identify commonalities. Where do they live?

What programs are they drawn to? What are their career goals? The more an institution understands about its audience, the more effectively it can craft digital advertising campaigns that resonate and drive action.

One of the biggest mistakes institutions make is bidding on broad, high-competition keywords that eat up budgets without delivering results. Terms like "MBA program" or "top business school" are expensive and often dominated by major universities with massive marketing budgets. Competing in that space is costly and ineffective.

Instead, the smartest institutions focus on long-tail keywords. A student searching for "best part-time MBA for working professionals" knows exactly what they want. They are further along in their decision-making process than someone who just types "MBA program" into Google. And purchasing these long-tail keywords can help you position yourself for those with needs that fit your program offering.

Another issue comes when institutions bid on their own name without a clear strategy. While it can be helpful to protect your brand name from competitor ads and build brand awareness, many institutions waste money bidding on keywords that students would have clicked on anyway through organic search. When digital advertising isn't centrally managed, the problem can get even worse. Imagine the central marketing team is running a PPC campaign for undergraduate recruitment, while a graduate program is running its own campaign with a different vendor. If both campaigns are bidding on the same brand name keywords, you're essentially bidding against yourself and driving up your own costs for no added value. This is called cannibalizing your own keywords, and it's one of the fastest ways to burn through a budget with nothing to show for it.

Now on top of all this, remember to keep your ad copy in mind. Even the best keyword strategy won't matter if the ad itself is generic and uninspiring. If an ad reads like every other institution's, including, "Top-Ranked Programs! Expert Faculty! Apply Now!", it won't stand out. Prospective students see dozens of ads like this every time they search, and most of them blend together.

Strong digital marketing speaks directly to a student's goals and pain points. A working professional considering an online MBA doesn't just want a degree. They want flexibility, career advancement, and an education that fits into their busy life. Where a high school student exploring undergraduate programs might care more about campus life, scholarships, and post-graduation job placement.

An effective PPC ad answers the *why* we discussed in the previous chapter. Why should a student choose this program over another? Why should they take action right now? The best ads cut through the noise by making an immediate connection with what matters most to the prospective student.

The landing page they end up on should reinforce this connection. Many institutions make the mistake of sending PPC traffic to their homepage or a generic admissions page. That's like inviting someone to an open house and then handing them a campus map with no guidance.

A high-converting landing page needs to do three things immediately:

1. Reinforce what the ad promised. If the ad was about an online MBA, the landing page should talk about that program specifically, not general admissions.

2. Make it easy to take action. Whether it's filling out a form, downloading a brochure, or signing up for a webinar, the next step should be clear and simple.
3. Build trust with the student. Testimonials, program details, career outcomes, and faculty highlights can help convince someone that this program is the right fit for them.

If a landing page is confusing, cluttered, or too general, the student will leave, and that click was just a wasted expense. But beyond clarity and design, there's a deeper strategic point here. Your campaign needs a dedicated landing page. Not your homepage and not your general program page. A landing page.

A true landing page is built for conversion. It should align perfectly with the ad or email that brought the student there, speak directly to the audience segment you're targeting, and guide them toward a single, clear call to action. Whether that's scheduling a visit, downloading a guide, or filling out an inquiry form, the page should make it incredibly easy to take that next step and hard to do anything else.

This is not the place for distraction. Strip out the top navigation. Remove the extra links. Avoid sending them into the institution's website maze where they can wander off into the student life section or start comparing unrelated programs. A good landing page is a "dead-end" in a good way. Every word, image, and button should point them toward the action you want them to take. Because if you've paid to get them there, this is the time to make it count.

Finally, remember a PPC campaign is never finished. It requires constant tracking, testing, and refining. Institutions should regularly analyze their campaign data to see what's working and what's not. If certain keywords aren't converting, they should be adjusted. If a particular ad gets a higher click-through rate than others, that messaging should be tested across different campaigns. This is where you can use AB testing (where you test the results of two similar, but lightly different messages) to help determine which headlines, images, and calls to action are most effective.

If an institution isn't using Google Analytics, UTM codes, and conversion tracking, they have no idea if their PPC spend is bringing in students. Let's take a closer look at the key performance indicators (KPI's) you should use.

KPIS FOR HIGH ED PPC MARKETING

In higher education marketing, throwing money at digital ads without tracking results is like driving cross-country without a gas gauge. Sure, you can keep moving forward, but at some point, you're going to run out of fuel, and you won't know when or why. That's why you need Key Performance Indicators (KPIs) to track your progress. They tell you what's working, what's wasting your budget, and where you need to adjust. When done well, KPIs become your dashboard of data and information to help make better decisions.

Not all KPIs are created equal, though. Vanity metrics, like impressions or even clicks, might make your campaign *look* successful. Unfortunately, many marketing agencies like to show off these numbers to their clients, claiming an effective campaign. But these numbers don't tell you if your efforts are actually bringing in students. Instead, you need to focus on the numbers that show whether your digital advertising is leading to real, tangible enrollments.

Here are some KPI's that should be on your radar:

Conversion Rate

Clicks mean nothing if they don't turn into actual leads. Conversion rate measures how many of the people who click on your ad take the next step, such as filling out an inquiry form, signing up for a webinar, or scheduling a call with admissions.

In higher education, conversion rates vary depending on the channel. Paid social campaigns typically convert around 2–2.5%, while paid search (when executed well) can reach closer to 5%. If your conversion rate is lower than 2.5%, that's a red flag. Either your landing page isn't compelling, the audience you're targeting isn't the right fit, or your ad lacks a clear call to action.

Organic website traffic, on the other hand, often sees much stronger conversion rates, ranging from 15–20%.[48] That means if you focus first on optimizing your website to convert inquiries and applications, you'll maximize the return on investment from paid search and social.

Cost Per Click (CPC)

CPC is a core metric in PPC and digital marketing. It tells you how much you're paying every time someone clicks on your ad. When institutions dive into PPC marketing, they often see high keyword costs and assume that's exactly what they'll pay per click, but that's not always the case. Keyword costs represent the estimated bid range for a search term based on competition and demand.

For example, a keyword like "MBA programs" might have a listed cost of $50 per click, but that doesn't mean every institution bidding on it is paying that amount. The actual cost per click (CPC) depends on several factors, including how well the ad is optimized, the advertiser's quality score, and the level of competition at any given moment.

An institution with a strong ad strategy might win a bid at a lower CPC, while another institution with a weaker campaign could end up paying more. So, while keyword costs give you a sense of how competitive a term is, your CPC is the real price you pay each time someone clicks on your ad.

In the higher education sector, the average CPC is around $2.10 as of 2025 depending on the source and specific keyword targeting.[49] But for high-competition keywords, costs can jump to $50 or more per click. If your CPC is high, but your conversion rate is low, you're paying premium rates for traffic that isn't turning into students.

Cost Per Inquiry (CPI)

Think of CPI as the price tag for getting a prospective student to raise their hand and say, *I'm interested.* It measures how much you're spending to generate a single inquiry, which is someone filling out a form, requesting more information, or calling your admissions team.

For higher education, the average CPI is around $140.[50] This means that every time you generate a lead through PPC, you're spending, on average, $140 to do so. That number fluctuates depending on the program, competition, and targeting strategy.

Why does this matter? Because not all leads turn into students. If your cost per inquiry is too high and your conversion rate is too low, you're spending a lot of money to *maybe* get one student through the door.

Click-Through Rate (CTR)

Your CTR tells you how effective your ads are at grabbing attention. It's the percentage of people who see your ad and click on it. A good CTR in higher education varies, but dynamic search ads (ads that adjust based on a user's search) have been shown to boost CTR by 20% compared to standard keyword-based ads.[51]

A low CTR means your ad isn't resonating, it could be the wrong audience, the wrong message, or just too much competition. A high CTR is a good sign, but only if those clicks lead to conversions.

Cost Per Acquisition (CPA)

CPI tells you how much it costs to get a lead. Cost per acquisition (CPA) tells you how much it costs to get an enrolled student, which applies to both online and traditional channels. This number is where a lot of institutions realize they've been playing the wrong game. If you're spending $140 per inquiry, but it takes twenty inquiries to get one enrollment, then your cost per enrolled student is actually $2,800.

On average, higher education institutions spend about $2,849 per enrolled student, but that varies widely:

- Undergraduate programs: ~$1,505
- Graduate programs: ~$3,804
- Non-credit programs: ~$599

If your PPC campaign isn't aligned with these benchmarks (or worse, if you don't know what your cost per acquisition is), then you're flying blind.

Keyword Costs

When it comes to PPC, not all keywords cost the same. Some are like prime real estate in downtown Manhattan, while others are more like a small shop on the edge of town. The more competitive the keyword, the higher the price tag.

For example, here are the average costs for different programs as of 2020:[52]

- MBA programs can cost over $45 per click.
- Business school can push past $50 per click.
- Online MFA might be under $20 per click.
- PhD in English can be as low as $5 per click.

The reason for these price differences? Competition. Business and law degrees tend to have a higher lifetime value (meaning students in these programs often pay more in tuition), so universities are willing to spend more per click to capture those leads.

Here's where strategy makes all the difference. As you can see, bidding on highly competitive keywords without a clear plan can quickly drain your budget, leading to high costs with little return. That's why focusing on long-tail keywords can be a game-changer. Not only do they cost less due to lower competition, but they also tend to convert at a much higher rate. In fact, across industries, long-tail keywords see an average conversion rate of 36%, far outperforming even the best-performing landing pages, which typically convert at 11.45%.[53] By prioritizing these more precise search terms, you can attract better-qualified leads while optimizing your ad spend.

If you have a good grasp of all these KPIs, you'll be able to navigate your PPC campaigns with confidence instead of guessing or relying on vanity metrics. Which means you can make informed decisions to adjust bids, refine targeting, and optimize ad performance.

THE MYTHS THAT KEEP INSTITUTIONS WASTING MONEY

Digital marketing has become such a dominant force in higher education advertising that many institutions blindly accept certain myths as truth, so I would like to address them here.

One of the biggest misconceptions is that a bigger budget automatically means better results. Too many institutions think that if they just had more money, they would get more students. But digital marketing isn't a vending machine where you put in a dollar and a student pops out. More money doesn't fix a flawed strategy. If an institution is already spending inefficiently by bidding on the wrong keywords, targeting the wrong audience, or failing to convert inquiries into enrollments, throwing more money at the problem only makes the inefficiency more expensive. While you might get a bump in a few more of the leads you are getting, your cost per acquisition will continue to rise.

Another myth? Every lead is a good lead. Institutions fall into the trap of thinking that if they are generating inquiries, their PPC campaign is working. But if those inquiries never turn into applications or enrollments, they aren't worth much. A hundred unqualified leads won't help an institution hit enrollment goals, but ten highly targeted, mission-fit leads might.

Quality beats quantity every time. Especially because not all leads are even real. Without the right filters and safeguards in place, your forms can be flooded with spam, bot traffic, or irrelevant international inquiries—none of which move the needle toward enrollment.

Then there's the idea that more keywords mean better performance. Institutions assume that if they just expand their keyword list, they'll increase their chances of attracting students. But more keywords don't necessarily mean more of the right students. In fact, bidding on too many keywords can lead to a bloated, unfocused campaign that burns through budget without delivering real results. The best PPC strategies aren't about having the most keywords—they are about having the right ones.

At the end of the day, PPC is a high-stakes investment. If an institution doesn't understand the full picture of digital marketing, it's easy to waste tens, or even hundreds, or thousands of dollars on campaigns that look good on the surface but don't actually lead to enrollments. The institutions that win in this space are the ones that question the myths, test their strategies, and evolve with the data.

ASK THE HARD QUESTIONS

I once worked with an institution that had a marketing budget of several hundred thousand dollars. That budget wasn't surprising as institutions often have varying sizes of marketing investments based on their budget and donations. What surprised me was where the money ended up. When I dug into their numbers, I found a huge chunk of their overall marketing budget had been line-itemed to a radio station's "digital marketing package" for $350,000.

When I asked if the institution was using radio ads, the answer was no. Instead, the radio station was running their digital marketing. That's where the red flags start. When traditional media outlets (like cable companies, TV stations, or newspapers) offer digital marketing services, it's often a desperate attempt to stay afloat. These organizations typically lack in-house digital expertise and end up outsourcing the work to freelancers on Fiverr or overseas teams who have no real understanding of the higher education industry.

Things got worse when I questioned this institution about their campaign results. They told me "We're getting tons of conversions every month!" When I asked how the radio station defined conversions, they were unsure. Turns out, when talking to the sales rep for the radio station, conversions didn't mean leads; it meant clicks.

Remember above, how I mentioned that a click is just someone clicking on your ad and doesn't point to conversions, inquiries, or acquisitions? This is why it's critical to ask the right questions when reviewing digital advertising metrics. If someone says your campaign is getting "tons of conversions," ask them:

- How do you define a conversion? Is it a lead, an inquiry, or just a website visit?
- What's the actual cost per lead? Are you paying $10 per inquiry, or $1,000?
- How many inquiries turn into enrollments? Leads don't matter if they never convert.
- How are we tracking student journeys to know what is working and what isn't?

The institutions who hand their digital advertising dollars to companies who aren't experts in higher education end up wasting the majority of their budget. I don't want that for you. This chapter should give you the knowledge you need to ask the hard questions to get the right results for your institution.

Marketing evolves faster than almost any other field, and that can create a lot of impostor syndrome. Which makes us hesitate to ask these hard questions, especially when we are speaking to someone who is supposed to be an "expert." It's easy to feel like you should already know all the answers, or that asking questions will make you look inexperienced. But the truth is, no one knows everything. And the people who get the best results are the ones who ask questions, even when they feel out of place doing so.

I've built my career on two simple phrases:

- "I don't know, but I'll find out."
- "I have a suspicion, but I'll find out."

Admitting that you don't know what you don't know is never a bad thing. I like to think of marketing the same way a general practice physician approaches medicine. A general practitioner doesn't specialize in cardiology, neurology, or orthopedic surgery—but they know enough to recognize a problem, ask the right diagnostic questions, and send a patient to the right specialist when necessary. In the same way, you don't need to be a digital marketing expert, but you do need to know enough to spot warning signs and recognize when you need a specialist.

TAKE ACTION

Understanding digital marketing is one thing, and applying it effectively is another. The following exercises and reflection points are designed to help you apply the ideas from this chapter to your unique context. Take time to work through them, either on your own or with your team, and use them as a springboard for meaningful conversations and actionable insights.

Reflective Questions

- What are our actual goals for PPC marketing? Are we just trying to get more inquiries, or are we focused on increasing enrollments? Do we have specific, measurable targets?
- Are we tracking our cost per inquiry and cost per enrolled student? Do we know exactly how much we're paying for each lead? How does this compare to industry benchmarks?
- Are we targeting the right students? Do we understand who our mission-fit students are and where they spend time online? Are we using long-tail keywords to attract students with high intent?
- What's our keyword strategy? Are we bidding on high-cost, high-competition keywords without considering their ROI? Have we tested different keyword strategies to see what works best?
- Are we relying too heavily on PPC? Do we have a diversified digital marketing strategy, or are we putting all our eggs in one basket? What other channels—SEO,

content marketing, social media—are we leveraging to attract students?

- Are we asking the right questions when working with external marketing providers? Do we fully understand the reports they provide? Are we assuming "conversions" mean actual leads rather than just clicks?
- Who is managing our digital advertising, and are they qualified? If we're bringing in someone to run PPC, can they show us their past successes? Can they clearly explain how they approach enrollment marketing, what tools they use, and which KPIs they focus on?

Action Steps

- Gather your current cost per inquiry (CPI), cost per enrolled student, keyword costs, and conversion rates. Compare them to industry benchmarks and see where you stand.
- Review your student personas and ensure that your PPC campaigns are targeting the right people in the right digital spaces.
- Refine your keyword strategy. Identify high-performing keywords and cut out underperforming ones. Test long-tail keywords that might yield better-qualified leads at a lower cost.
- If you're not already tracking cost per inquiry, cost per enrolled student, and conversion rates, start now. Set up Google Analytics 4 (GA4), UTM codes, and conversion tracking to measure campaign effectiveness properly.

- If an agency or internal team is managing your PPC, ask them what their definitions mean. Are "conversions" actual leads, or just clicks? Check that their reported metrics are aligned with your enrollment goals.
- If you're hiring or working with someone to manage PPC, demand proof of success. They should be able to demonstrate past wins, explain how they improved digital advertising performance, and clearly articulate their approach to enrollment marketing. A portfolio alone isn't enough; ask them to show their expertise.
- Make sure PPC isn't your only student acquisition method. Invest in SEO, content marketing, email nurturing, and social engagement to build a sustainable long-term pipeline.

7

WEBSITE MARKETING: THE WEBSITE IS NOT A CATALOGUE

"We sell feelings, status, and connection, not tasks or stuff."
—Seth Godin

A STUDENT RESEARCHING COLLEGES clicks onto your website, hoping to get a feel for what life at your institution is really like. They're excited, maybe even a little nervous, because this decision will shape their future. For traditional students, they want to picture themselves walking across campus, sitting in classrooms, making friends, and stepping into opportunities that will set them on the path toward their dream career. For adult and grad students, they want quick benefits to assure that their needs are understood. But if what they find instead is dense program descriptions and a list of course requirements, delivered in cold, academic language, you've lost the moment. The spark of connection fades, replaced by the sense that this might not be the place for them.

They scroll for a few more seconds, trying to find something that resonates, but nothing jumps out. The excitement fades. The uncertainty grows. Without an emotional connection or a clear reason to stay, they close the tab and move on to the next institution on their list.

This happens *all the time.* Year after year, research confirms that an institution's website is the top influencer in a student's enrollment decision.[54] Yet many institutions make the mistake of treating it like a digital course catalog; packed with information, but completely lacking in inspiration. They take the program descriptions written by faculty, copy them onto the website, and assume that's enough. I understand why it happens. The logic seems sound. After all, the catalog contains all the relevant information about the institution's offerings, but an academic catalog is not marketing.

A catalog is written for a specific purpose. It's a reference guide, built to outline academic policies, degree requirements, and course structures in precise, technical terms. It's designed to be used by people who are already inside the institution (students, advisors, faculty) not by prospective students who are still trying to decide where to go. A website, on the other hand, should be focused on why a student should want to earn that degree at this particular institution.

For prospective students, the website is often their first real interaction with an institution. A well-structured, engaging website has the power to spark excitement and build confidence in their decision. But if students encounter only dense program descriptions and course requirements, they may struggle to connect with the experience your institution offers. Without that sense of connection, they're more likely to disengage and continue their search elsewhere.

The challenge many institutions face is that websites are often built to serve multiple audiences (faculty, current students, alumni, and donors) making it easy for enrollment messaging to get buried under necessary but transactional details. While facts and figures are important, they don't always speak to the aspirations that drive a student's decision to apply.

A student doesn't choose an institution because the business curriculum is "comprehensive and interdisciplinary" or because the engineering program requires a hundred-twenty credit hours. They choose it because they can picture themselves pitching a startup idea in a business incubator, working alongside top professors on real-world engineering projects, or landing an internship with a company that could launch their career. They need to see students like them thriving on campus, hear alumni stories about how this institution shaped their future, and understand—within seconds—why this is the place where they will belong, grow, and succeed.

The key to an enrollment-driven website is understanding that students are looking to be inspired. They want to know if this institution will open doors for them, if the degree will lead to the career they envision, if they'll be supported along the way. The question running through their minds isn't, Does this institution offer a degree in my field? It's, *Will this institution get me where I want to go?*

The institutions that understand this will shift their website away from information dumps and toward engagement. They focus on telling their story, showing what makes them unique, and illustrating the real-world outcomes their students achieve.

They don't just state that they offer an engineering degree, they show engineering graduates who have gotten hired by top companies. They don't just list tuition costs, they explain how students afford their education and what their financial aid options look like. They create an experience that is inviting, persuasive, and most importantly, focused on the student's future.

THE MOST CRITICAL PARTS OF YOUR WEBSITE

One of the biggest mistakes institutions make with their websites is believing that every department, faculty member, and administrator should have equal say in its content. This leads to websites that are designed by committee, and the design process is slow, bureaucratic, and filled with competing voices that dilute the message. Even worse, in some cases, the responsibility for content is spread across different departments, resulting in a fragmented, inconsistent experience.

But your website isn't an academic project, it's your most powerful marketing tool. And the truth is, prospective students don't visit every page on your site. In my experience, the three most important pages for their decision-making are the home page, the tuition or cost-to-attend page, and the majors/programs page. But within those, certain sections carry the most weight. The about section tells them if they will fit in, the academics section (including the majors list and details on the program pages) answers the fundamental question of whether your institution offers what they're looking for.

Each of these pages serves a distinct purpose, but together, they shape the initial perception of your institution. The homepage sets the tone, the about page builds trust, and the academics page answers the fundamental question of whether your institution offers what they're looking for. Done right, these pages guide students toward the next step in their journey. Let's analyze the elements that should be included in each one.

The Homepage: Create Connection

The homepage is the first thing most prospective students see when they visit your website, and in just a few seconds, they're trying to answer three critical questions: Am I going to fit in here? Do you have my major? Can I afford this?[55] A well-designed homepage doesn't try to provide every answer at once, but it does acknowledge the most important concerns, provide an emotional hook, and guide visitors to explore further.

The best homepages immediately immerse the visitor in the experience of the institution. A dynamic visual—ideally a background video—can showcase campus life, engaged students, and hands-on learning in a way that static text never could. This video, positioned in the first section of the page, acts like a billboard. It should instantly convey what makes the institution distinctive. In a 30-second loop, quick visual cuts can highlight the energy and personality of the institution including classroom discussions, research projects, athletic events, or international study opportunities. If a picture is worth a thousand words, a video is worth a million. Without sound, without narration, it should give students a glimpse of what life at this institution feels like.

Beyond that first impression, the homepage should guide exploration. Some worry that long pages will overwhelm visitors, but today's students are used to infinite scrolling experiences. They naturally expect to keep moving downward, uncovering more information as they go. Instead of treating the homepage as a brief introduction, think of it as a curated experience where you can layer the content in a way that keeps students engaged while allowing them to discover what's most relevant to them.

This is where institutions can highlight their most popular programs, showcase a few student or alumni testimonials, and weave in key statistics that reinforce their brand. If affordability is a major selling point, don't bury that information under layers of navigation. List the average cost after financial aid right there on the homepage, and if needed, use an asterisk[56] to provide additional details. Parents especially are looking for those signals of value.

While some institutions devote valuable homepage space to news and events, that kind of content isn't what prospective students are looking for when they first visit. If it's included at all, it should be placed toward the bottom, where it won't distract from the bigger message. What should be front and center, however, are your calls to action. The most effective homepages make it obvious what steps a student should take next—requesting more information, starting an application, or scheduling a visit. These should be visually distinct, easy to find, and available across all devices.

The About Page: Who You Are and Why You Matter

For many students, the about page is where they determine if they "fit" at your institution. They've landed on your website, maybe through a search engine or a recommendation, and now they want to know more. What kind of institution is this? What does it stand for? Will I belong here? This is where the about page plays a pivotal role.

While marketing departments typically handle the about page, it needs to be more than just a long-winded history lesson or a generic mission statement. Instead, it should be scannable, informative, and immediately useful to prospective students and their families.

One of the best ways to structure an about page is to include an "at a glance" section, which is an easy-to-read snapshot of your institution's defining characteristics. Think of this as the cheat sheet for your institution. A prospective student (or parent) should be able to glance at this section and quickly understand key details, like:

- Faith affiliations, if applicable
- Information about the town or city your institution is in
- Historical background around how your institution came to be
- The vision that drives your institution forward
- Class sizes and faculty-to-student ratios
- The percentage of male versus female students
- Any other defining features that shape the student experience

These facts allow students to filter their expectations of college life against what your institution offers. A student coming from a small high school might be more comfortable with a lower student-to-faculty ratio. Another might be drawn to the location, especially if your institution is in a unique setting like a major metropolitan area or a scenic rural town. These details help them build a mental picture of what life at your institution would be like.

Beyond stats and facts, the about page is also a great place to reinforce the mission and values of your institution. Why do you exist? What is the larger vision that drives your institution forward? Every institution has a story, and this is where you get to tell it. For institutions with a rich history, this is an opportunity to highlight your roots. For newer institutions, it's a chance to showcase the innovation and energy behind your founding.

A well-designed about page should also include a "Welcome from the President" section as a way to humanize your institution. Prospective students want to feel connected to the leadership of the institution. A personal, authentic message from the president, ideally accompanied by a photo or video, sets the right tone. It signals that this institution is led by real people who care about students' success.

Additionally, listing key leadership figures including the cabinet, the board of trustees, and other senior leaders, gives visitors a sense of the people behind the institution. Who is making decisions? What backgrounds do they come from? This adds depth and credibility, particularly for parents or donors who want to see the expertise and vision behind the institution.

The Academics Page: Make It Student Centered

It's easy to see how academic program pages often end up as extensions of the course catalog. After all, faculty spend years refining program details and all that information is important. But when a prospective student arrives on your academics page, they aren't looking for the fine print just yet. They're trying to answer a much simpler question: *Does this institution offer what I want to study?*

This is where many institutions unintentionally create friction. Instead of a clear, student-friendly list of majors and programs, the academics page is often organized by institution or department, requiring students to know, for example, that a Criminal Justice degree falls under the School of Social Sciences or that Environmental Science might be part of a Sustainability and Ecology Division. But most high school students (and even their parents) don't think in terms of academic departments. They're looking for their major in a way that makes sense to them.

One of the easiest ways to make your academics page more user-friendly is to list majors, minors, and certificates alphabetically, rather than by department. When a student visits your website, they should be able to scan the page and quickly find their area of interest. This simple shift reduces frustration, keeps them engaged, and allows them to move deeper into your site via hyperlink to the program page rather than bouncing to another institution's page when they get frustrated.

In an effort to stand out, some institutions rename programs in ways that feel more modern or unique. But while Administrative Justice might sound more sophisticated than Criminal Justice, a prospective student searching for "best criminal justice programs" might not realize that's what you offer.

This doesn't mean institutions shouldn't differentiate their programs, just that the differentiation should happen on the program page itself, rather than in the main listing on the academics page. There's plenty of room to explain how your approach to Environmental Studies is different or why your Digital Systems & Intelligence Technologies program stands out on the page that is dedicated to that program. But the initial navigation should be clear, direct, and easy to understand.

Once a student clicks into a program page, that's where the real work begins. This is a page that often serves as the first (and sometimes only) introduction to your institution. If a student searches for "Best Nursing Programs in Ohio" and lands directly on your Nursing Program page, what they find there will shape whether they decide to explore further or move on.

This is why program pages should be outcome-focused, with course details as a supporting element, not the other way around. Students absolutely need to know the course sequence and graduation requirements, but these details matter more after they've connected emotionally and can see the value of the degree in their lives. The initial focus should be on answering questions and tapping into the motivations that spark engagements, such as:

- What kinds of careers do students go into after graduation?
- What percentage of alumni are working in this field?
- Where have past graduates landed jobs? Did they stay local or work abroad?
- What internship or hands-on learning opportunities are available?
- What salary ranges can they expect in this field?

For parents, these questions are especially important. Some institutions even include salary projections based on labor market data or alumni earnings, which helps families understand the long-term value of the degree.

Beyond statistics, students and families want to see success stories. This is where alumni profiles and testimonials can make a deep impact. Featuring a graduate who has used their degree to land an exciting job or make a difference in their field provides a sense of credibility and aspiration. When a prospective student sees someone like them thriving after graduation, it helps them envision their own future at your institution.

Another great way to build confidence is to include faculty profiles on program pages. Parents, in particular, want to know who will be teaching their child. Showcasing faculty credentials, research interests, and even short videos or quotes can help humanize the program and make it feel more approachable. This is especially meaningful for faith-based institutions, where families often want to know more about the faculty's values and background beyond the typical CV.

Finally, every program page should have a call to action that guides students toward the next step you need them to take. Whether it's scheduling a visit, requesting more information, or applying, there should always be a clear and compelling next step offered throughout the program page.

When these three key pages (the homepage, about page, and academics page) are built with prospective students in mind, they directly impact enrollment. A well-crafted homepage grabs attention and encourages deeper exploration, an about page helps students self-identify as a fit for your institution, and an academics page makes it easy for them to find their program and understand the opportunities ahead. When these pages are engaging, and outcome-driven, students stay on your site longer, take action more frequently, and move through the enrollment funnel with greater confidence.

TRANSACTIONAL CONTENT VS. ENGAGING CONTENT

A great way to identify transactional content is to step into the mindset of a prospective student and ask, *does this content tell me what the institution offers, or does it help me see how going to this institution would benefit me?*

Transactional content is often dry, fact-heavy, and imperson-al—it lists course names, degree requirements, or accreditation details without providing context or emotional connection. It might read, "Our business program offers a rigorous curriculum with courses in finance, marketing, and management," rather than, "Gain real-world business experience through internships, mentorships, and hands-on projects that prepare you for leadership roles."

Transactional content tends to focus on *what* exists, while engaging content focuses on *what it means for the student.* If the language on your website feels passive, overly technical, or sounds like it was copied straight from the academic catalog, it likely isn't engaging enough to influence a prospective student's decision. A simple way to evaluate your content is to ask if the content creates excitement, aspiration, or a sense of belonging in the reader. If the answer is no, it may be time to refine the messaging to make it more emotionally compelling.

Instead of just saying, "98% of our students graduate," go further, and say, "Our graduates go on to launch careers in top companies, earn competitive salaries, and make an impact in their communities." The graduation rate is a feature, but the real selling point is how that degree translates into a better life.

Indiana's Ivy Tech[57] (the largest community college in the nation) captured this idea with an ad featuring graduates throwing their caps in the air, paired with the message: *At Ivy Tech, the goal isn't graduation day. It's a better every day after.*[58] That message resonates because it speaks directly to why students pursue higher education in the first place.

We make decisions with our hearts first, then use our heads to justify them later. That's why the best marketing doesn't just rattle off features, it tells a story. It taps into what we want, what we're afraid of, and what we're hoping to become. In his book *StoryBrand,*[59] Donald Miller breaks this down into a practical framework that helps businesses simplify their messaging. The core idea is that your audience is the hero, and you're the guide showing them how to solve a problem or reach a goal. In higher education marketing, the student is the hero, and the institution is the guide. The website's job is to show how the institution can help them overcome obstacles and reach their goals through every stage of the student journey.

This concept is reinforced in the book *The Psychology of Marketing*[60] by Harinder Singh Pelia, which explores a range of psychological triggers that influence decision making, such as: urgency, fear of missing out (FOMO), social proof, reciprocity, and the power of storytelling. Pelia explains how these triggers shape perception and behavior, showing why people are naturally drawn to opportunities that feel time-sensitive, endorsed by others, or personally relevant. In the context of higher education marketing, these principles play a significant role in how students engage with a college website and whether they take the next step.

A great website doesn't manipulate emotions but instead strategically builds momentum by helping students recognize the opportunities available to them and encouraging them to take action. Instead of simply listing an admissions deadline, an engaging website might frame it as, "Apply by December 1st to be considered for our top merit scholarships. Your future starts now." This small shift in language turns a passive detail into an active prompt that creates a sense of urgency without feeling forced.

Beyond deadlines, FOMO can also be created by showcasing student experiences and success stories in a way that makes prospective students feel like they don't want to miss out on what's happening at this institution. Featuring alumni who have landed dream jobs, students who have studied abroad, or undergraduates working on groundbreaking research projects paints a vivid picture of what's possible, making prospective students think, *I want that experience too.*

In the end, the goal is simple: Don't just inform. Connect.

Prospective students are looking for more than information. They are looking for a story they can see themselves in. When your content moves beyond facts and taps into emotion, identity, and aspiration, it invites students into a relationship—not just a transaction.

PUT YOUR WEBSITE ON A DIET

Many institutional websites start with a clear vision, but over the years, they grow into sprawling ecosystems. It's easy for a site to become bloated over time, with years of accumulated content piling up until the structure becomes overwhelming.

While there's no magic number, for small to medium-sized institutions, keeping a website between five-hundred and a thousand pages is generally ideal. I would also make this recommendation for individual colleges within larger institutions. This isn't a fast-and-strict rule, as larger institutions such as flagships and regional public institutions often have deeper, more specific content requirements that naturally expand their site size. Anything beyond those needs, however, tends to dilute the user experience, making it harder for prospective students to find what they need.

A big part of trimming a website down is recognizing what content belongs on the public site and what is better suited for internal systems. Learning Management Systems (LMS),

Student Information Systems (SIS), and other internal platforms exist for a reason—there's no need for course syllabi,
faculty meeting notes, or department-specific materials to be
housed on the main website. Once this kind of content is shifted
into the right internal tools, it becomes much easier to focus
the website on what truly matters for prospective students and
families.

Analytics can be an invaluable resource in this process. By
looking at which pages are actually being visited, institutions
can make informed decisions about what to keep, what to
consolidate, and what to remove. In one case, we worked with
an institution that wanted to get their site under five hundred
pages. At the time, they had nine-hundred-fifty pages, which
was far more than they needed. Surprisingly, three hundred of
those pages belonged to the biology department alone, even
though biology wasn't even one of their most popular majors.
The faculty had been using the website as a storage space for
class materials for years, and while that may have served their
internal needs, it created an inaccurate representation of the
institution. A prospective student landing on the site might
assume this institution was a *major* STEM powerhouse, when
in reality, other programs were far more central to its identity.

Managing a college website is no small task. It serves multiple audiences, spans hundreds (if not thousands) of pages, and
often involves input from numerous departments. With so many
voices in the mix, it's easy to lose sight of who truly owns the site
and what that ownership entails.

This is where strong website governance becomes key. Without
clear policies and oversight, institutional websites quickly become
fragmented, inconsistent, and confusing for users. IT teams play a
critical role in maintaining the infrastructure, uptime, and security

of the site, but they aren't content strategists. Decisions about what content belongs on the site, how it's presented, and how it supports the institution's goals should be made by those who specialize in messaging, branding, and user experience.

In other words, the marketing department should own the website.

When content decisions are left to chance or divided between too many stakeholders, it becomes nearly impossible to maintain a cohesive, strategically aligned presence. Marketing teams are best equipped to approach the website from a student-first perspective. They understand how to frame messaging, guide the user journey, and ensure that every page reflects the institution's mission, values, and enrollment priorities.

However, if marketing sits within advancement, there's often a natural tendency to focus on donor engagement rather than prospective students on the website. This is when I have seen the website become a branding tool or a public relations hub rather than an enrollment engine. The messaging leans more toward fundraising appeals, press releases, and institutional news rather than guiding prospective students toward action.

This is why regular collaboration between marketing and enrollment is critical. The website should reflect the needs of prospective students first. If marketing and enrollment aren't working together to shape the site's content, structure, and messaging, then the institution is likely losing prospective students without even realizing it.

For institutions that prefer a more distributed authorship model, establishing clear guidelines is essential. A website shouldn't be a free-for-all where different departments or colleges create pages however they see fit. Without structure, this leads to inconsistency, both in branding and in functionality.

That's how you end up with rogue pages full of Comic Sans, outdated faculty bios, or program descriptions that don't align with the rest of the institution's messaging.

A great solution for maintaining consistency is leveraging AI-driven tools and branded templates. Custom AI models trained on the institution's voice, branding, and messaging can help departments craft content that fits within the overall marketing strategy. The use of a good CMS (content management system) to manage consistency is a must. Additionally, tools like Canva can provide your institution with templates for graphics, pre-approved content frameworks. Other project management tools can provide a structured approval process to ensure that while departments have the ability to contribute, the marketing team retains final say to ensure consistency and alignment with institutional goals.

When you put your website on a diet, you're not just cutting pages, you're reclaiming purpose. A lean, student-focused site is easier to navigate, easier to manage, and far more effective at driving enrollment. With the right balance of structure and flexibility, your website becomes a powerful, conversion-ready asset that continually supports your goals.

WEBSITE REDESIGN PITFALLS TO AVOID

A website redesign is a major investment, but if not approached strategically, it can create more challenges than it solves. We've seen institutions spend significant resources on a new website, only to realize too late that critical enrollment elements were overlooked. In one case, we were brought in after a redesign where the institution had completely omitted admissions from the main navigation, making it nearly impossible for prospective students to figure out how to apply. These kinds of mistakes happen when institutions don't test their site with real users—prospective students—before launch, or they hire an agency who doesn't specialize in the higher education space.

While creativity is important, navigation is not the place to reinvent the wheel. Students compare institutions side by side, and they expect a familiar structure that makes it easy to find essential information. Differentiation should come through messaging, visuals, and storytelling, not through confusing navigation that creates friction.

Another common oversight is the cost of maintaining a website. In the day-to-day rush of priorities, institutions don't always have the bandwidth to assess whether they're overpaying for things like hosting, content management systems (CMS), or agency retainers for ongoing updates. We've worked with institutions that spend far beyond the industry average simply because they've never sought competitive quotes or questioned whether their pricing aligns with standard benchmarks.

At the same time, institutions that try to cut costs too aggressively often end up with a poorly designed website that doesn't meet industry standards. If an institution hires a local freelancer (or a board member's nephew) to save money, the result may be a site that fails to support enrollment goals.

The best approach is to balance expense with expertise. Investing in a website designed by professionals who understand higher ed ensures that the final product meets both student expectations and industry benchmarks. If your institution is unsure whether you are making the right website decisions, it's worth seeking expert advice![61]

TAKE ACTION

Now is the time to take a step back, assess your institution's digital presence, and ensure that your website is designed to engage, inspire, and convert. The following exercises and reflection points are designed to help you apply the ideas from this chapter to your unique context. Take time to work through them, either on your own or with your team, and use them as a springboard for meaningful conversations and actionable insights.

Reflective Questions

- Take a closer look at your student journey. Are you presenting content in a way that prioritizes prospective students' needs, aspirations, and decision-making processes?
- Review the friction your perspective students face. Are your calls to action (request info, schedule a visit, apply now) clear, prominent, and easy to access across all key pages? Are academic programs listed in a way that makes sense to students (alphabetically rather than by department)? Are you using standardized, easy-to-understand program names instead of confusing or overly creative labels? Have you tested your website navigation with prospective students to ensure they can find what they need quickly?
- Does your homepage immediately communicate who you are, what makes your institution different, and why students should choose you?

- Are you leveraging video, testimonials, and real student success stories to create an emotional connection?
- Is your website managed by marketing with a focus on enrollment, or is it controlled by IT or advancement with a different set of priorities?
- Have you reviewed your analytics to see what content is actually being used, what's outdated, and what needs to be optimized—or removed?
- Are your decisions based on data, or are redesigns driven by internal preferences without input from prospective students?
- Have you vetted your website vendors to ensure they truly understand the needs and best practices of higher education?
- If you're using a distributed authorship model, do you have the right guardrails in place—like branding guides, content templates, or AI tools—to keep everything consistent?

Action Steps

- Conduct a website audit. Start by reviewing analytics to identify underperforming pages, outdated content, and high-exit points where students drop off. Then assess whether academic program pages effectively showcase student outcomes and career pathways. Check the homepage, about page, and academics page for clarity, engagement, and strong calls to action.
- Conduct usability testing by asking prospective students to navigate the site and report on any confusion or frus-

tration. Gather feedback from current students about what worked (or didn't) when they were researching institutions.

- Ensure every key page has a clear next step, whether it's requesting more information, scheduling a visit, or starting an application. Make sure CTAs are prominent, easy to find, and mobile-friendly.
- Remove unnecessary pages or consolidate information to keep the site focused and easy to navigate. Move internal content (faculty resources, syllabi, meeting notes) to internal systems like LMS or SIS platforms.
- If your website is controlled by advancement, IT, or another department, start conversations about transitioning ownership to marketing. Ensure enrollment and marketing teams meet regularly to align website strategy with student recruitment goals.
- If working with an agency, ensure they have experience in higher education and understand best practices.
- Finally, evaluate whether your website's infrastructure and technology are the right "Goldilocks" fit—not overbuilt with costly, unnecessary tools, and not underpowered in ways that limit functionality and user experience.

8

PERSONA MARKETING: YOU ARE NOT THE AUDIENCE

"If you do not know how to ask the right question, you discover nothing."
—W. Edwards Deming

IF YOU HAVE WORKED in higher education for any amount of time, you've likely encountered a moment where a well-thought-out marketing plan was presented to the leadership, only for a board member, faculty leader, or even the president to chime in with, "I don't really like that." Maybe it was a campaign that used slang or humor to connect with Gen Z, only to be met with a concern, and the question, "Is this academic enough?" Maybe it was a TikTok video that was gaining traction online but got pulled because someone in leadership thought it wasn't "serious" enough.

Or maybe—like me—you've seen website copy scrubbed of every contraction because an academic proofreader was determined to enforce a formal writing style, even though the entire point of the campaign was to sound friendly and conversational.

The problem isn't that presidents, board members, or faculty lack valuable insights. Many of them are deeply invested in the institution's success, and their expertise is invaluable in other areas. But when it comes to marketing, their opinions often stem from personal preferences rather than audience insight, and that's where things go off track.

If you are not a prospective student, your opinion about what "works" in marketing is, at best, an educated guess. Yet, too often, campaigns are shaped (or worse, scrapped) based on the preferences of people who will never be on the receiving end of the messaging.

Much of this problem stems from how we frame our discussions. If you ask a board member, "Do you like this campaign?" they will give you an honest answer based on their own experiences, preferences, and feelings. They might say, "I don't get this meme" or "I don't like the casual tone" or "This doesn't feel right to me."

But the university leadership is not your audience. So, the better question would be, *Do you think this will be effective for our target audience?"*

That subtle shift in the question itself changes the answer deeply. Now, instead of evaluating the campaign based on personal taste, the conversation shifts to strategy. The focus is no longer on whether leadership likes the approach, but on whether it will work for the people we are trying to reach.

A few years ago, I worked with an institution on a social media campaign specifically designed for Gen Z. It used humor, quick cuts, and text overlays, all formats that were performing well with prospective students at the time. Within days of launching, engagement skyrocketed. The campaign was capturing attention and driving website traffic.

Then, a board member saw one of the videos and said, "This doesn't feel academic enough." Despite data showing the campaign was effective, and despite the fact that students were engaging with it, the leadership team got nervous. The videos were pulled, the campaign was scrapped, and what replaced it was a more "formal" approach, one that blended in so seamlessly with every other school's messaging that it barely made a ripple online.

How many higher ed marketers have had to fight for the simplest, most audience-friendly decisions? How many website redesigns have been held up because a faculty member wanted to rewrite every paragraph in academic language? How many campaigns have been watered down into bland, forgettable messaging because someone in leadership couldn't see past their own perspective?

This is the battle marketing leaders fight every day.

Marketing isn't about internal consensus; it's about *external connection*. As leaders, it's important to remember that marketing isn't designed to reflect your personal tastes or preferences. It's designed to resonate with prospective students. That means sometimes setting aside what we like in favor of what works. Because when we treat marketing as an internal approval process, we risk diluting its effectiveness.

Let's break down the mindset shift needed to separate personal preference from effective strategy, navigate these conversations, and ensure your marketing remains focused on the right audience, not the people signing off on it.

THE VANITY SPEND

During a marketing budget evaluation I conducted with a Vice President of Marketing at a large institution, I flagged an unusual line item. Twenty percent of her budget was allocated to billboards and bus wraps. Given the institution's target demographic and marketing goals, it didn't add up. Digital campaigns, social media engagement, and search engine marketing were driving inquiries, so why was such a significant portion of the budget being spent on outdated, broad-reach advertising?

She sighed and leaned back in her chair. It wasn't about effectiveness, she explained. Those ads weren't generating inquiries, and they certainly weren't converting students. Even the brand awareness wasn't the most strategic. Their sole purpose was visibility for leadership. If the president and board members didn't see marketing efforts out in the world—on their daily commutes, in airports, or plastered on city buses—they assumed the marketing team wasn't doing anything at all.

So, despite knowing that money could be better spent elsewhere, she kept approving the billboards and bus wraps. Not because they worked. Not because they brought in students. But because they kept leadership off her back.

Her team had run digital campaigns with precise targeting—ads placed where prospective students actually were, on platforms like TikTok, YouTube, and Instagram. Those campaigns had performed well, generating high engagement and leading directly to inquiries. But instead of celebrating those successes, she was constantly defending them to the board, who saw none of the digital efforts firsthand.

She had tried to explain to the board that if her team was marketing correctly, they wouldn't be seeing the targeted ads at all. But they didn't trust her. Moments like this are much more than a misallocation of funds. In truth, these moments are a lack of trust in marketing leadership. And the reality is, she is right. If your board members and faculty are seeing your marketing, something is likely wrong. Good lead-generation marketing isn't designed to reach the boardroom. It's designed to reach prospective students. So, a university president shouldn't be seeing digital ads for undergraduate enrollment in their LinkedIn feed. If they are, it means the marketing team is wasting ad spend targeting the wrong people.

A well-run campaign should result in:

- More applications from mission-fit students
- Higher engagement from prospective students and parents
- Increased campus visits and inquiries
- A clear ROI on marketing spend

What it shouldn't be measured by is whether or not the board personally sees the ads. Even brand awareness data should reflect prospective students and influencers. Brand awareness has its place, but in today's limited budgets, it's often a luxury rather than a primary driver of spend. Now, leadership should absolutely ask where marketing dollars are going. But those metrics should be tied to effectiveness, not visibility. Instead of asking,

"Where do I see our marketing?"

They should be asking:

"Where is our marketing being seen by prospective students?"
"How is it performing?"
"What is our cost-per-inquiry and cost-per-enrollment?"

We need to avoid vanity marketing. Or marketing for the sake of visibility, not audience reach. At the end of the day, it truly is an unnecessary cost imposed when leadership doesn't trust marketing to do the job they were hired to do. Just as Patrick Lencioni said in his book *The Advantage*,[62] "The healthiest organizations are those in which politics are reduced to a minimum and people feel free to focus on their work and contribute to the success of the organization without having to navigate a political minefield."

WHEN THE BOARD DOESN'T UNDERSTAND MARKETING

Boards exist to provide oversight, governance, and strategic direction. Many of them are successful business owners, executives, or leaders in their respective fields. The problem is that most of them don't understand higher education marketing. And when decision-making is guided by personal bias, past experiences in unrelated industries, or sheer gut instinct instead of marketing expertise, it leads to bad marketing investments that waste time and money.

Here are a few key ways boards misunderstand marketing which I continually see. I bring these up not to point a finger, but to help you understand what should be avoided. Let's take a closer look at each of these four mistakes:

1. "My Nephew Builds Websites in His Basement."

Board members love to analyze contracts and proposals, but when they don't understand the value of professional marketing services, they see price tags without context. A marketing agency submits a proposal for a new website redesign, backed by audience research, UX testing, and strategic positioning. The board sees the cost and balks.

"Why are we paying this much? My nephew builds websites in his basement. Why don't we just hire him?"

This happens more often than you'd think. To someone without marketing experience, a website is just a collection of pages with a navigation bar and some images. What they don't see is how a well-designed website strategically guides prospective students toward inquiries, applications, and enrollment. When leadership prioritizes cost savings over quality, institutions end up with ineffective, outdated, or amateurish websites that do little to drive actual engagement.

2. "I Just Don't Like It."

This is one of the most common critiques marketing teams hear from faculty, board members, and even internal leadership. It's almost always rooted in personal preference. Maybe someone doesn't like the color scheme, the font, or the phrasing in a headline. I once had a faculty member push back on an entire campaign because they didn't like serif fonts.

But that font wasn't chosen at random. I let them know we chose this font objectively, not subjectively, because the data proves that serif fonts are often associated with security, tradition, and credibility,[63] which is why you'll see them in branding for banks and law firms. The choice was based on what the research showed would resonate with the target audience.

Marketing shouldn't be guided by subjective taste. It should be grounded in objective strategy. You might not personally like a design, a phrase, or a campaign concept. But if the data supports it, and it connects with prospective students, that's what matters.

3. The Vice Chairman Runs an Ad Agency—and Wants the Contract.

I once worked with an institution where the Vice Chairman of the board owned an ad agency. It didn't take long before he suggested that, rather than hiring an outside marketing firm, his agency should take on the advertising work.

On paper, it might have seemed like a convenient solution. But this was a massive conflict of interest. When leadership is allowed to funnel institutional contracts into their own businesses, it undermines objectivity, strategy, and accountability. Instead of making decisions based on what's best for student recruitment, marketing budgets end up serving personal profit, and that's when institutions start burning money on ineffective tactics.

4. "It Worked for My Business, So It Should Work for the Institution."

One of the most common (and most dangerous) mistakes board members make is assuming that because something worked in their business, it will work in higher ed marketing. I once worked with a small, rural faith-based college where a board member looked to the local tractor dealership. The dealership was thriving, and he attributed that success to regional TV ads and billboards placed all over town. So naturally, he insisted that the institution do the same.

"It worked for us. Why wouldn't it work for you?" he asked. Because higher education is not the same as selling tractors.

A tractor dealership sells to everyone in the community because the vast majority of the community worked in agriculture. A small Bible college does not. The product, audience, and buyer journey are completely different. Throwing marketing dollars into general advertising just because it worked for a local business means wasting budget on people who will never consider enrolling.

This is why targeted marketing matters. Instead of broadcasting to everyone, successful institutions identify their mission-fit students and market to them in the right places. It's the difference between standing on a street corner with a megaphone and having a personal conversation with someone already interested.

When board members start making marketing decisions based on personal experience, gut feelings, or their own business successes, institutions lose sight of what actually works. Luckily, there are a few key ways to overcome these issues.

TEST YOUR MARKETING WITH PROSPECTIVE STUDENTS FIRST

When a board doesn't have faith in marketing tactics or understand much about them, it becomes the marketing leader's duty to provide proof of concept.

During a marketing budget evaluation with an institution, I asked their Vice President of Marketing how they gathered insights on what was working. Did they have data? Student feedback? Or were they just running campaigns and hoping for the best? She nodded and told me about a practice she had picked up from a colleague at Ball State University (BSU).

Every year, during orientation, Mary Barr, a former marketing leader at BSU, would grab a group of ten to twelve brand-new students, order a few pizzas, and sit them down for an informal conversation. She'd ask them about their journey to Ball State. What had led them there? What messages stood out to them? Which marketing efforts did they remember?

In essence, she had created a focus group of students who had just been through the enrollment process to tell her exactly what had worked. All it had cost her was a few pizzas.[64]

There was nothing particularly complicated about this, and yet, it was one of the most effective strategies I'd heard. Instead of making assumptions, she was getting direct insights from the people who mattered most. By doing this every year, she ensured that she wasn't relying on outdated information. Marketing trends shift quickly, especially with Gen Z. What worked last year might not work this year. A message that resonated with last year's seniors could fall flat with this year's. So instead of guessing, she asked.

This approach isn't limited to orientation. If you wanted feedback, you could simply walk into the dining hall at lunchtime, sit down at a table, and start asking questions. What do students think of the last ad campaign? What emails did they open? What made them click on something? A five-minute conversation in a campus dining hall could give more actionable insights than hours spent in a conference room speculating.

Even artificial intelligence could be used as a tool for perspective. If you asked ChatGPT to act like a seventeen-year-old in your region looking for a college, what would it say? How would it respond to different messaging styles? This isn't a replacement for real conversations with students, but it could serve as an additional lens to view how messaging might land with younger audiences.

Too many institutions build marketing campaigns in a vacuum. They hold brainstorming meetings, come up with ideas they think will work, put the campaigns together, and launch them without ever testing them on the people they were supposed to attract. Then, when a campaign doesn't land, they are left wondering why. Sometimes, the problem isn't the execution but the foundation itself. If the messaging wasn't built on student insight, it was already at a disadvantage.

There is another advantage to this method. If a president or board member questions a campaign, you can bring student feedback directly to the table. That way, if leadership says, "I don't really like that" you have proof of concept to back up why your campaign worked this way. This data shifts the conversation from personal preference to actual data.

Now, if your institution has different audience segments, such as adult learners, transfer students, or graduate students, you need to gather these marketing insights from each of those groups separately. An eighteen-year-old fresh out of high school won't make decisions the same way as a thirty-two-year-old returning to school after a decade in the workforce. Their motivations and needs are different, and the way they see and consume media is different. Create a strategy that allows you to test your marketing campaigns with all relevant groups so you can be most effective within each one.

Strategically Place *and* Position Your Campaigns

Finding your audience's watering holes (the platforms they naturally gather on) is only half the battle. TikTok, Instagram, YouTube, and even Reddit are teeming with your prospective students. But just showing up in these spaces doesn't guarantee attention. People go to watering holes for entertainment, inspiration, and connection, not necessarily to shop for colleges. If your content doesn't stand out, it gets scrolled past like every other ad.

That's why gaining attention inside the digital watering hole is what actually matters. To do that, your content needs to make someone pause mid-scroll. It needs stop-imagery, unexpected copy, or a headline that gets a double take. Think bold visuals. Conversational hooks. A touch of humor or mystery. You need to find a way to stand out in a feed full of influencers, memes, and trending sounds. And you only have a second or two to earn that attention.

But capturing student attention on TikTok isn't the same as convincing a parent reading a printed viewbook. This is where many institutions trip up. They try to repurpose the same message across every platform without adjusting for context. A playful, slang-filled post might crush it on Reels, but drop that same tone into a mailer, and the message will feel off. It's not about what's right or wrong—it's about what fits the audience and the medium.

Parents want reassurance. They want to know if their child will be safe, supported, and well-prepared for a career. They're not looking for punchy slang or trending sounds, they are looking for substance. That's why the same campaign needs different expressions depending on the placement. Show the board how you've accounted for that, and you'll face far less resistance in getting bold work approved.

Creativity is only as effective as its aim. Speak the language of your audience, in the place where they're most likely to hear it, and say it in a way that makes them stop and listen.

EDUCATE DECISION MAKERS

One of the most overlooked responsibilities of a marketing leader is educating stakeholders. You can't expect board members, faculty, or even some administrators to understand higher education marketing if no one has ever taken the time to explain it to them. People don't know what they don't know, and in many cases, they don't even know what questions to ask.

If you're a university president, part of your job is to educate your board on how marketing, enrollment, and communications actually work. The same applies to marketing leaders working with cabinets, general boards, or enrollment committees. Without a shared understanding of how modern marketing functions, decision-making becomes reactive, opinion-driven, and frustratingly ineffective.

Too often, marketing teams are left justifying strategies to people who don't have the context to evaluate them properly. This is where things break down. A board member may look at a budget proposal for digital marketing and dismiss it outright because they don't see the value, not realizing that a well-optimized paid search campaign could generate far more inquiries than a traditional media buy. Someone from faculty may object to a campaign's tone without understanding the audience research that went into it. These conflicts don't stem from bad intentions. They stem from a lack of shared language and knowledge.

One way to bridge this gap is by giving board members resources that help them get up to speed. A book like *Chasing Mission Fit* can provide them with a working foundation in higher education marketing, so when key decisions come up, they can engage in discussions with a basic understanding of how enrollment strategies work. For an even more collaborative approach, the *Chasing Mission Fit Study Guide* can be used with the cabinet or leadership team to work through key concepts together and align on strategy. The more educated they are, the less friction there will be when it comes time to approve budgets, campaigns, and messaging strategies.

Frankly, most board members will appreciate this. They don't want to feel out of the loop. They want to be brought into the conversation, to understand the facts, and to make informed decisions. If that doesn't happen, they might default to gut reactions and personal opinions.

This is also why a university president needs to be the number one ally of the marketing team. If the president doesn't fully buy into the marketing strategy, the entire operation is left exposed. Without that top-level support, every decision becomes a fight. Faculty members push back on messaging, board members second-guess campaigns, and marketing teams find themselves constantly defending their work rather than executing it. Or worse yet, the marketing team is reduced to an institutional Kinkos taking orders and making things look prettier by Monday.

When the board or faculty starts questioning decisions that are based on real data and sound marketing strategy, the president needs to step in and reinforce why those decisions are being made. If that doesn't happen, marketing leaders are left playing defense, wasting time putting out fires instead of focusing on what actually drives enrollment.

This is the difference between an institution where marketing thrives and one where it constantly struggles to prove its value. In the first scenario, leadership understands marketing's role, trusts its experts, and creates an environment where strategy is driven by data, not personal preference. In the second, marketing is a constant uphill battle, with every campaign subject to scrutiny from people who don't understand the fundamentals of how it works.

WHEN THE BOARD IS YOUR AUDIENCE (AND YOU NEED TO PRESENT MARKETING TACTICS)

Marketing teams often make the mistake of assuming that a great campaign will speak for itself. But when you're presenting to a board, a presidential cabinet, or faculty leadership, you're not talking to students, and you're certainly not talking to other marketers. You're talking to decision-makers who think in terms of institutional priorities, revenue impact, and long-term strategy—not fonts, social media trends, or the psychology of color choices.

Dale Carnegie, in *How to Win Friends and Influence People*,[65] put it best: "The only way to influence people is to talk in terms of what the other person wants." That quote should be your guiding principle every time you present marketing to leadership. If you walk into a cabinet meeting and start by explaining why you chose a particular shade of blue for your social media ads, you've already lost them. They don't care about design choices. They care about outcomes.

When presenting a campaign to a presidential cabinet, the first thing you should talk about is revenue impact. University leadership doesn't measure success in impressions or engagement rates; they measure it in tuition dollars or increased giving. Before showing a single creative asset, frame your campaign around how it will drive enrollment, increase applications, and ultimately impact the institution's financial health. If you're speaking to faculty leadership, shift the focus to academic reputation and student success. Show how the campaign will attract mission-fit students who will thrive, graduate, and contribute positively to the community.

If you're presenting to the board, take a high-level, strategic approach. Boards care about long-term sustainability, institutional growth, and public perception. They want to know how this marketing strategy aligns with the institution's vision, mission, and competitive standing.

This means adjusting the language and focus of your presentation based on your audience. Imagine you're unveiling a new digital campaign aimed at increasing applications from first-generation college students.

- If presenting to the president's cabinet, you start by showing projected application growth, expected yield rates, and how this campaign supports strategic enrollment goals.
- If presenting to faculty leadership, you focus on how the messaging supports access and inclusion while still maintaining academic excellence.

- If presenting to the board, highlight how this initiative enhances the institution's long-term reputation as a place that provides upward mobility for students.

Each group sees the same campaign but framed in a way that speaks to their priorities. This will help you because marketing at its core is storytelling. Seth Godin, in *All Marketers Are Liars*,[66] wrote, "Marketing is no longer about the stuff that you make, but about the stories you tell." That holds true even when you're presenting to leadership. Your job is to tell the story of why it matters.

If a campaign's goal is to increase applications among under-represented students, don't just talk about numbers—tell the human story. Bring in real voices from prospective students who struggle to see themselves in higher education. Show how the campaign bridges that gap, making college feel accessible and achievable. A well-placed student testimonial, one that explains how a specific marketing message helped them make their decision, can do more to convince leadership than a deck full of data points.

Finally, remember to read the room. One of the fastest ways to lose an audience is to focus on the wrong details for the setting. Let's say you're unveiling a new brand campaign. You might be tempted to lead with the creative by explaining the psychology behind the color choices, the nuance of the typography, or how the campaign aligns with modern design trends.

My advice? Don't. The campaign might be beautifully designed. The messaging might be fresh and creative. Once you've framed the campaign in terms of goals and results, then you can get into the details of execution. By that point, you've already established credibility.

If leadership feels like they're being asked to validate a campaign they don't fully understand, they will default to personal, subjective opinions. That's when you get comments like, *"I don't like that font"* or *"Could we use a different color?"* because those are the only things they feel equipped to weigh in on. But if they understand the strategy first, their feedback will be more aligned with actual marketing goals rather than personal preferences.

When leadership sees marketing as a means to achieve their objectives, rather than just another department asking for budget approval, everything becomes smoother. That is the moment marketing stops being an uphill battle and starts being a collaborative process.

TAKE ACTION

Speaking to the right audience is powerful, whether you're focusing on the student or presenting to the board. The following exercises and reflection points are designed to help you apply the ideas from this chapter to your unique context. Take time to work through them, either on your own or with your team, and use them as a springboard for meaningful conversations and actionable insights.

Reflective Questions

- Are your campaigns designed for prospective students, or are they shaped by internal preferences? Have you tested your messaging with actual students before launching it?
- Are there areas where leadership's visibility demands (billboards, print ads, general awareness campaigns) are diverting budget from high-impact strategies?
- Have you provided board members, faculty, and administrators with a basic understanding of how modern higher ed marketing works? Does leadership understand why digital strategies matter, or are they still expecting traditional marketing tactics?
- When pitching campaigns, are you focusing on design and creativity—or on institutional goals like enrollment growth and revenue impact? Could you better frame marketing discussions around data and effectiveness rather than subjective preferences?

Action Steps

- Set up an informal focus group during orientation to ask new students about their enrollment journey.
- Walk into the dining hall, sit with students, and ask what marketing messages stood out to them when choosing a college.
- Test messaging with different audience segments—traditional undergrads, transfer students, adult learners—to refine your approach.
- Provide resources or assign reading (*Chasing Mission Fit* is a great place to start) to create a common understanding of marketing's function within leadership.
- Schedule quarterly marketing briefings with leadership to present campaign performance and insights. Set clear expectations about how marketing success is measured beyond personal visibility or subjective opinions.
- Identify any marketing dollars being spent purely to make leadership feel comfortable rather than to reach prospective students. Ensure that leadership understands why they shouldn't be seeing your ads—because if they are, they're not reaching the right people.
- Meet with leadership regularly to align on these messaging priorities, consider how what you are doing might be perceived, and offer strategies to alleviate any friction or roadblocks ahead.

9

ENROLLMENT MARKETING: A FERRARI CAN'T PULL A BOAT

"Once you really accept that spending money does not equal happiness, you have half the battle won."
—Ernest Callenbach

HAVE YOU EVER SEEN SOMEONE buy a sports car only to realize it's completely impractical for their needs? Maybe they live in a snowy climate, or they have a family of five and need more seats. Or worse, they need to tow a boat. A Ferrari is impressive, no doubt. It turns heads, makes noise, and looks great in the driveway. But if you hook a trailer to the back of it, you're in for a rude awakening.

Higher education leaders often make this same mistake when building their marketing teams. They assemble a group of incredibly talented creatives, including award-winning design-ers, masterful videographers, and branding experts who produce stunning work. The problem is those creatives don't always know how marketing in higher education works. They may craft a gorgeous brochure, a viral social media post, or a breathtaking video, but if those assets don't contribute to enrollment goals, what's the point?

Too often, leaders hire based on specialized skills rather than strategic understanding. But in a world where marketing and enrollment are deeply interconnected, it's not just about what someone can create or what awards they have won. It's about whether they know how to drive results. I'd hire a journalist who understands content strategy over a designer with a shelf full of awards any day, and that is coming from someone who started their career as a designer.

The goal isn't to get the best of the best on your marketing team, because the best of the best might not understand higher education marketing. Even the most talented marketers can struggle if they rely on tactics that don't fit higher education.

NOT EVERY STRATEGY TRANSFERS

Success in another industry does not automatically translate to success in higher education marketing. But that doesn't stop people from trying to force square pegs into round holes.

I've seen it repeatedly. A board member or executive assumes that because a tactic worked in their industry, it will work just as well for student recruitment. "I run a car dealership, and billboards work great for us. Why don't we do that for our institution?" Or they see a trend, like marketing on Snapchat, without realizing that students don't want to be sold to in that space. Then they pour resources into areas where students aren't even looking.

The higher education sales cycle is fundamentally different from most industries. It's not transactional. It's a long, emotional, highly considered decision. A billboard might create awareness, but it won't nurture a student through their decision-making process. A trendy social media campaign might generate engagement, but if it's not aligned with how students explore, apply, and commit to institutions, it's just noise.

Interestingly, I've noticed that professionals who transition from healthcare into higher education tend to adapt more easily. Why? Because they're already accustomed to navigating both B2B and B2C marketing. Just like in healthcare, where you must engage both doctors (B2B) and patients (B2C), higher ed marketing has to balance communication with parents, students, counselors, and internal stakeholders. Which means the marketing goal becomes focused on a strategic multi-touch approach that nurtures prospective students over time.

If you want real success, you can't just apply whatever worked in another industry. You need to understand the nuances of higher education marketing, or risk pulling your boat with a Ferrari.

THE SHIFT TO ENROLLMENT-FOCUSED MARKETING

Even the most talented professionals can struggle if they don't understand the nuances of higher education marketing. In one meeting with a client, the creative director proudly announced that their main project was "a brochure for admissions," and couldn't understand why he was getting pressure to get it done so quickly as it was only early September. He didn't know the industry term viewbook, the core piece of collateral admissions reps carry during travel season, nor did he understand the urgency of finalizing the piece in time for recruitment season.

For anyone outside the industry, that might seem like a small slip. But in higher ed, viewbooks are foundational tools that have to be ready before September, when admissions reps hit the road for the fall travel season—visiting high schools, attending college fairs, and meeting families face-to-face. Without those materials in hand, reps are flying blind.

What struck me wasn't just the terminology gap, but the attitude. The creative director was confident, even smug, that he would "get to the brochures when he got to them," with no sense of urgency around the enrollment cycle. He didn't know that timing is everything, or that missing fall travel means missing your best window to connect with prospective students.

That's the danger when you bring in talented marketers from outside industries. In corporate or small business settings, sales can happen year-round. But in higher ed, enrollment follows a strict cycle with immovable deadlines. If your marketing team doesn't understand that rhythm, they can't align their work to the actual realities of recruiting students. They don't know what they don't know.

If your marketing team doesn't understand the enrollment funnel, the sales cycle, or the critical dates in the academic year, how can they develop effective marketing strategies? It's not enough to have creative talent. Your team needs to understand how and when students make decisions and how marketing fits into that process.

This knowledge gap isn't surprising when you consider the history of marketing in higher education. For decades, marketing departments in universities weren't focused on recruitment. They sat within the advancement office. Their main job was producing alumni magazines and fundraising materials. That made sense thirty years ago when those were the primary communication channels for institutions. But things changed when computers came along.

In the early 90s, as websites became essential and institutions started developing admissions materials targeted at prospective students, advancement teams found themselves out of their depth. Digital marketing wasn't just about designing print materials anymore. Suddenly, these teams had to:

- Build and manage institution websites
- Create and execute digital marketing campaigns
- Handle social media engagement
- Run Google Ads and optimize for search engines

This was an entirely different skill set, and many institutions weren't prepared for it. Instead of growing their teams or investing in specialized training, they simply tried to do more with the same people. Marketing teams meant to handle alumni relations were now expected to drive enrollment without the necessary expertise.

Over the last ten to fifteen years, higher education leadership has started recognizing this problem. Many institutions have finally moved marketing out of advancement and into the revenue-driving C-suite, typically under a Chief Marketing Officer (CMO) or under a Vice President of Enrollment Management and Marketing. This shift has allowed marketing to focus on selling the institution rather than just maintaining its image.

A growing number of schools have found success by splitting marketing and communications into two complementary functions:[67]

- Communications—Focused on branding, PR, and institutional reputation.
- Enrollment Marketing—Aligned with admissions, using marketing strategies to drive student recruitment.

This model allows marketing to work together with enrollment teams, applying the same level of expertise you'd expect in any other competitive industry, which is a critical shift.

The next phase of this evolution can be seen at larger universities that have built internal *brand studios*—full-service agencies that handle all marketing and communications for the institution. Purdue University,[68] for example, has gained national recognition for this approach. Their brand studio model helped land them on *Fast Company's* "Brands That Matter" list, and it was the only higher education institution included.

But there isn't just one way to structure marketing in higher education. Smaller institutions may benefit from dividing communications and enrollment marketing into complementary functions, while larger universities with more resources can elevate marketing into a cabinet-level role, often through a chief marketing officer who oversees a unified brand strategy. Purdue's brand studio is an example of this corporate-style model.

The lesson here isn't that every school should look like Purdue, but that courageous leadership and a strategic approach to marketing—whether through specialized enrollment teams, integrated brand studios, or a mix of both—create a competitive advantage. What matters most is that marketing informs strategy (rather than simply reacting), ensuring decisions align with the institution's goals.

THE ENROLLMENT FUNNEL

One of the biggest gaps I see in higher education marketing is a lack of understanding about how students move through the decision-making process. Many marketing teams are exceptional at creating content, running campaigns, and building a brand, but without a clear grasp of the enrollment funnel, they risk missing the bigger picture. And it's not their fault. Higher education marketing is complex, and for years, many teams were built with a focus on communications rather than student recruitment. But as marketing plays an increasingly critical role in enrollment, understanding this funnel is no longer optional.

Whether you're in admissions, marketing, or leadership, having a solid grasp of how students move from awareness to application to enrollment allows you to make smarter decisions, create more effective strategies, and ultimately, drive better results. That being said, let's take a closer look at each stage in the enrollment funnel.

Prospect

At the very top of the enrollment funnel is what's traditionally known as *Search Marketing*, and no, this doesn't refer to search engine marketing. Here, we're focusing on the traditional undergraduate (TRAD) enrollment context—other audiences, such as adult learners, graduate students, or transfers, often require different techniques, timelines, and outreach strategies. Historically, this term has meant purchasing lists of potential students who have registered for standardized tests like the ACT or SAT. Colleges and universities would buy tens of thousands of student names from these test providers in their target recruitment regions and demographics. From there, they'd launch outreach campaigns through direct mail, phone calls, and text messages, introducing themselves and encouraging students to inquire or apply.

But this strategy is rapidly shifting. We're now facing what some have called the search cliff, which is a term popularized by Jenny Petty, Vice President of Marketing, Communications, Experience, and Engagement at the University of Montana, who was the first and most prominent voice to identify the trend.[69] The COVID-19 pandemic accelerated a movement that was already underway—test-optional admissions. More and more institutions have made standardized tests optional, which means fewer students are taking the ACT and SAT. And if fewer students take these exams, that means fewer names for colleges to buy. Institutions that have traditionally relied on purchased names to fill the top of their funnel are finding themselves in uncharted waters.

The big question now is: *How do we build awareness and attract students without relying on these lists?*

Search marketing was just one way to move students into the inquiry phase, but it was a dominant strategy for decades. Now, institutions need to rethink their approach. The focus must shift toward stronger brand awareness, digital engagement, and more sophisticated content strategies that naturally draw students in. Institutions can't just introduce themselves through a purchased name anymore. They need to be present where students are already looking and provide value long before a student ever inquires.

As we move through the enrollment funnel, it's important to recognize that the way we generate interest is evolving. The old playbook is changing, and institutions that don't adapt will struggle to maintain a steady pipeline of prospective students. With the traditional search marketing model shifting, institutions need to lean into other ways of attracting prospective students, such as college fairs and pipeline programs.

College fairs have long been a staple of student recruitment, offering a chance to meet students face to face, answer their questions, and put an institution on their radar. But beyond fairs, some institutions have developed more immersive recruitment experiences in what I'd call *watering hole opportunities*. These are structured programs designed to introduce students to an institution in a meaningful way, creating a natural path toward application.

Take Rose-Hulman Institute of Technology as an example. They host a summer camp for high school juniors interested in engineering, allowing students to experience their campus, faculty, and programs firsthand. By the time those students head into their senior year, they already have a connection to Rose-Hulman, and that makes them much more likely to apply.

Other institutions tap into community organizations, church camps, and youth leadership programs as recruitment pipelines. This can also include what are known as "feeder institutions," such as faith-based high schools, STEM focused charter schools, or community colleges for transfer students. Any place where students gather is an opportunity to spark interest and begin building relationships. But to move students from *interest* to *action*, institutions need to give them a reason to take the next step.

That's where incentives come in. Whether it's an application fee waiver, priority scholarship consideration, or early access to housing choices, giving students a tangible reason to move to the next step of the funnel can make all the difference. The key is making the process feel seamless and valuable, so when the time comes, students see your institution as their first choice.

Inquiry

When a student lifts their hand, whether at a college fair, a summer camp, or another recruitment event, they move from being just a prospect to something much more valuable: an inquiry. This is the moment when they go from being a name on a list to someone who is actively interested in your institution. They've shown intent. They're saying, "Tell me more."

The problem I've seen is too many institutions don't treat inquiries as the opportunity they are. Instead of nurturing these students, engaging them, and earning their trust, they rush to push them straight into the application process. But Gen Z and Gen Alpha students are savvy. They don't want to be sold immediately. Asking them to apply the moment they express interest is like proposing marriage on the first date. It's too soon, too fast, and likely to drive them away.

Instead, this is where the real work of marketing begins. Institutions need to focus on wooing students by building a relationship, demonstrating value, and helping them see why your institution could be the right fit. The goal shouldn't be to push applications. Instead, the goal should be to offer them relevant content, personalized outreach, and an experience that makes them feel seen and valued. Which will then earn you the right to ask for the application.

A welcome email from a faculty member, a quick text from an admissions counselor, or even a short video featuring current students sharing their experiences are all great examples of outreach at this stage. Invite students to virtual info sessions, campus visit days, or even social media groups where they can interact with current students. Targeted content, like "Day in the Life" videos, internship success stories, and financial aid breakdowns, helps inquiries visualize themselves on campus. Gen Z students expect authenticity and connection, and institutions that take the time to nurture these relationships will stand out.

Application

From August through December, colleges enter what is commonly known as "application season." This is when students take the critical step of filling out their applications—usually online, though if any institution is still relying on paper applications, it's time for a serious conversation. The process typically takes twenty to thirty minutes and often includes multiple requirements including an essay on why the student wants to attend, letters of recommendation from teachers or mentors, and high school transcripts. On the surface, it seems straightforward, but many students start their applications but don't finish them simply because of the overwhelming requirements.

Which means we need to treat the application processes as what it is. A series of steps, instead of one action. Some students submit the form but forget to send in their transcripts. Others get stuck waiting on recommendations or lose momentum before hitting submit. This creates a backlog of incomplete applications. Effectively giving you a list of students who have already shown strong interest but can't move forward in the process.

This is where "moves management" comes into play—a strategy often used in fundraising to move donors from one level of giving to the next. The same concept applies to the enrollment funnel. Our goal is to move students forward and sell them on completing their application. Institutions that are strategic in this phase actively encourage students to complete their application through marketing campaigns. They use reminder emails, personalized outreach from admissions counselors, and even incentives like fee waivers or early housing selection to push students toward completion.

Acceptance

Typically, between October and March (depending on the institution), students start receiving acceptance letters. This marks the beginning of "yield season," and this is an exciting moment! But it's also a key point in the enrollment funnel. Just because a student has been accepted doesn't mean they'll enroll. Institutions that stop engaging at this stage risk losing students to other institutions that continue building the relationship.

The best institutions treat acceptance as an opportunity to reinforce a student's excitement and move them toward the next step, which is submitting their deposit. A well-crafted acceptance package can make all the difference. This should include more than just a letter. Some institutions send branded swag, create social media engagement opportunities (like a "*University Name* Said Yes" campaign), and invite students into exclusive admitted-student communities.

At the same time, in the U.S., this is also typically FAFSA season, where students and families are making financial decisions. Institutions need to be proactive in helping students navigate financial aid and ensuring they understand their options, deadlines, and potential scholarships. When they do, they further create value and build relationships with the potential students.

Deposit and Enrollment

Between December and May, students move from accepted to deposited. Most institutions require a deposit to hold a student's place, even if it's a small, refundable amount. This step signals that the student is serious about attending. Smart institutions use this as a lever to drive early commitment, offering perks like priority housing selection, early access to meal plans, or exclusive student events. By getting students to put some "skin in the game," you create a sense of investment that keeps them connected and moving toward enrollment.

But even after a student deposits, they are still in decision-making mode. Competing institutions are still reaching out, and financial concerns can cause hesitation. This is a time for continued engagement where institutions nurture deposited students, offering personalized communications, invitations to admitted student events, and access to online communities where they can connect with future classmates.

A student isn't fully committed until they've taken the final steps—registering for classes, attending orientation, and actively engaging with their new community. So, it's your goal to actively create exciting, community-driven experiences that reinforce a student's decision.[70]

Orientation, class registration, and campus visits are opportunities to solidify commitment. Gen Z and Gen Alpha students thrive on shared experiences, so designing orientation events that foster friendships, community, and belonging will increase retention. In fact, "Visit" is often one of the three primary calls to action on an institution's website, right alongside "Inquiry" and "Apply," because of its proven impact.

A 2021 survey of Chief Enrollment Officers found that "95% of respondents consider campus tours important in a prospective student's decision to enroll, with 86% rating them as "very" or "extremely" important." Among private institutions, this figure rises to 91%.[71] Which means institutions that prioritize engaging, dynamic campus experiences where students feel welcomed, supported, and excited will see stronger yield rates.

At this stage, the goal is no longer about convincing students to choose your institution. It's about making them feel at home before they even arrive. The more connected they feel, the more likely they are to show up in the fall, ready to begin their college journey.

Melt Mitigation

Between May and August, registered students start to melt. Even after they've deposited and enrolled, doubt creeps in. Some start questioning whether they want to go to college at all. Others reconsider their choice of institution, thinking about deferring for a year or getting a job instead. Even the strongest incoming class will experience some degree of summer melt.

This is where strategic summer engagement becomes essential. Institutions that continue nurturing students during these months can significantly reduce melt and ensure students actually show up in the fall. The key is to keep students feeling excited, connected, and reassured about their decision.

One of the best ways to do this is by reinforcing social belonging and helping students establish a peer network before they ever step on campus. Institutions can create online communities, group chats, and admitted student meetups where future classmates can connect. The more friendships a student builds, the more likely they are to follow through with enrollment.

Marketing efforts should also keep the momentum going. Institutions can send content that builds anticipation, like dorm move-in guides, sneak peeks of campus life, or student stories that showcase what makes the institution special. Even simple check-ins in the form of personalized emails, texts, or videos from faculty or student leaders can make a huge impact.

Arrival

The moment a student arrives on campus is one of the most critical points in their journey. First impressions matter, and universities that treat arrival as more than just a logistical process will see higher retention and stronger student satisfaction. This is the first customer service experience for students, and it sets the tone for their entire college experience.

Some universities go all out, mobilizing an army of student volunteers to help unpack suitcases, set up dorm rooms, and make new students feel at home. Others focus on large-scale orientation events, ensuring students immediately feel like part of a community. One of the most overlooked yet impactful moments is the transition when parents leave. It's an emotional and overwhelming time for new students. The best institutions handle this with intention, offering structured events, Resident

Director (RD) introductions, and group activities that make students feel welcomed, rather than abandoned.

Many institutions also host a separate parent presentation, often called the "official break-up," to help families transition smoothly. This reassures parents while reinforcing that their student is in good hands.

But arrival is just the beginning. The first few weeks are crucial in making sure students integrate, build friendships, and find their support network. Institutions that prioritize community-building activities, mentorship programs, and intentional social experiences during this time will see far fewer students slipping through the cracks.

Census Day & Retention

Roughly two weeks after classes begin, colleges and universities conduct a Census Day. This is the point where institutions take an official count of enrolled students, which is the number that will define the institution's enrollment for the year. But while Census Day marks the end of the enrollment funnel, the work of retention is just beginning.

Even after students arrive on campus, some may begin to second-guess their decision. Maybe they struggle to adjust, feel disconnected, or face unexpected challenges. Institutions often experience a final wave of melt within the first few weeks, losing students who decide to transfer or withdraw before Census Day.

This is why early intervention is key. Universities should closely monitor engagement, class attendance, and student well-being in these critical first weeks. Advisors, RDs, and faculty can play a crucial role in identifying students who may be struggling and providing support before they leave. Small actions, like checking in, offering resources, or connecting students with mentors, can make a big difference in keeping them enrolled.

This, paired with ongoing communication campaigns, such as encouraging emails or text messages, can reassure students and reinforce their sense of belonging. Sharing student success stories from upperclassmen who navigated similar challenges helps normalize the adjustment period, while promoting campus resources like tutoring, mental health services, and student organizations ensures students know where to turn for support. Marketing can also foster community-building by featuring student spotlights, social media takeovers, and interactive campaigns that encourage engagement, helping new students form connections.

Remember, retention is a campus-wide effort, and when marketing works in tandem with admissions, student affairs, and faculty, it helps create an environment where students feel seen, supported, and motivated to stay. If institutions don't continue nurturing their students past Census Day, they risk losing them before the next term even begins.

This is why marketing shouldn't stop after enrollment. Institutions need to maintain engagement with their students, reinforcing the value of education, the opportunities ahead, and the sense of community students have built. Retention-focused marketing can highlight student success stories, career pathways, and the personal growth that happens in college. Simple but intentional touchpoints, like check-ins from advisors, social events, and academic support initiatives, can help students feel invested in staying.

The institutions that succeed in retention are the ones that continually remind them why they chose to stay.

Wrapping Up the Enrollment Funnel

At every stage of the enrollment funnel, students need to be guided, encouraged, and convinced to take the next step. From the first moment a student expresses interest to the day they walk across the graduation stage, institutions have countless opportunities to engage them. In fact, I believe there are close to 67 touchpoints an institution can make with a student throughout their academic journey and beyond. (Interested in the list? Scan the QR code for the blog. A  well-timed email can remind a student why they applied in the first place, a meaningful campus event can strengthen their commitment, and a proactive check-in from an advisor can make the difference between a student staying or leaving.

THE CHALLENGE OF STEALTH APPLICATIONS

One of the biggest shifts in higher education enrollment is the rise of stealth applicants. These are students who apply without ever appearing in an institution's funnel beforehand. Their names weren't purchased, they never inquired, and they had no formal interaction with the institution until they submitted an application. Understandably, this trend frustrates admissions teams because it makes predicting and planning for enrollment much more difficult.

But just because the institution didn't interact with these students before they applied doesn't mean they weren't influenced by outside conversations. Today's prospective students rely heavily on peer-driven decision-making and online communities that institutions often don't have visibility into. Platforms like ZeeMee (a social networking app for prospective college students) play a huge role in shaping student choices. A student might see their friends discussing a certain institution on ZeeMee, visit the website, and decide to apply without ever formally entering the institution's inquiry pipeline.

Another major driver of stealth applications is the Common App, which allows students to apply to multiple institutions with just one form. This only impacts institutions that choose to participate in the Common App and pay the associated fees, but for those that do, the effect is significant. The average student today applies to fourteen different colleges, often selecting institutions they hadn't researched in-depth. This creates extra work for admissions teams, as they now need to nurture and engage applicants who may have applied with little knowledge of the institution itself.

The mistake many institutions make is treating stealth applicants the same way as students who have been nurtured through the traditional enrollment funnel. But these applicants require a different strategy. They aren't like prospects casually browsing a car dealership; they're like a buyer walking in with a checkbook in their back pocket, ready to make a decision.

Stealth applicants represent a warmer lead, and institutions should capitalize on that momentum. Institutions need separate marketing campaigns specifically designed for these applicants, helping them quickly learn about the institution's culture, values, and differentiators. Instead of assuming they already feel connected, admissions teams should act as if they are introducing the institution for the first time, because in many ways, they are.

With the right approach, stealth applicants can be converted into enrolled students at a high rate. The key is recognizing where they came from, why they applied, and what they need next to feel confident in their decision.

TRAINING ADMISSIONS TEAMS TO SELL THE INSTITUTION

If an institution is going to be successful in recruiting students, it's not enough to have great marketing, the admissions team needs to know how to sell the institution. This is an area where many institutions fall short. Leadership needs to understand that hiring people who lack experience in higher education recruitment—and then failing to train them properly—simply isn't going to work.

Let's think about this from the students' perspective. Higher education is often the most expensive investment a person will make in their life, and it's typically being sold to them by a twenty-three-year-old who has little experience in sales or the weight of the investment itself. Institutions rely heavily on recent graduates as admissions counselors, yet many times they don't provide them with the sales training necessary to succeed. As a result, turnover in these roles is massive—the average admissions recruiter only stays in the job two years.[72] That kind of instability is a problem when an institution's enrollment numbers depend on these young, inexperienced salespeople.

I have seen this firsthand where I've put together a highly effective marketing campaign, filled the funnel with strong leads, and driven student interest, only to find out that the admissions team didn't follow up properly. A prospective student raises their hand, expresses interest, and admissions calls them three times.

If they don't answer? That's it, the team moves on. But recruitment doesn't work like that.

Building relationships takes persistence and commitment. I recently landed a contract with an institution that was fifteen years in the making. I met the decision-maker, built a relationship, followed him through three different institutions, and finally closed the deal. Someone joked that I "don't quit," but they're right. My work is how I survive. Why would I walk away from a relationship that could turn into something valuable? Yet, many admissions teams lack this mindset. It's not necessarily their fault—they don't know what they don't know—and they're often being paid a small salary to do a job they were never properly trained for.

The truth is that recruitment isn't just about the admissions team. It's a campus-wide effort. Success in student enrollment depends on a coordinated approach, which includes having an emotionally compelling website, a strong alumni network that speaks positively about the institution, and faculty and staff who leave a great impression on visiting students. Every interaction matters. Without strong leadership ensuring that these elements work together, institutions will continue to struggle with enrollment, even if they have a great marketing funnel in place.

BUILDING THE RIGHT TEAM FOR ENROLLMENT SUCCESS

As a leader, understanding how to hire strategically, foster a strong team culture, and provide professional development opportunities is essential for reaching enrollment goals. Without clear direction and the right expertise, even the most well-intentioned teams can struggle to make an impact.

I recently worked with an institution that was facing significant enrollment challenges. They were doing their best, but they didn't have the right framework in place to guide their decisions. Instead of seeing results, they were feeling frustrated and asking questions that weren't leading them in the right direction. They didn't know what they didn't know. My recommendation? Invest in professional development and bring in the right expertise to help navigate the complexities of enrollment marketing. Sometimes, having an outside perspective or additional training can make all the difference in aligning efforts with outcomes.

When institutions take the time to equip their teams with the right knowledge and resources, they set themselves up for long-term success. Instead of trying to pull a boat with a Ferrari, they have the right vehicle in place, ensuring their efforts lead to real, measurable results.

TAKE ACTION

As a leader in higher education, your ability to build a strong enrollment and retention strategy starts with asking the right questions and taking intentional steps to refine your approach. The following exercises and reflection points are designed to help you apply the ideas from this chapter to your unique context. Take time to work through them, either on your own or with your team, and use them as a springboard for meaningful conversations and actionable insights.

Reflective Questions

- At what stage in the enrollment funnels (both traditional undergrad as well as adult and graduate) does your institution lose the most prospective students? What strategies do you have in place to address this?
- How well does your team understand the prospective student decision-making process? Where are the gaps in knowledge that could be filled with professional development or strategic hires?
- Does your admissions team have the skills and training necessary to effectively nurture prospective students? If not, what professional development opportunities could help them improve?
- How persistent is your follow-up strategy with inquiries and applicants? Are prospective students receiving enough engagement to guide them toward enrollment?

- How does your institution currently address summer melt? What additional strategies could be implemented to keep students engaged before the fall semester?
- How strong is the sense of belonging on your campus during the first few weeks of school? What initiatives or programs could be introduced to ensure students integrate successfully?
- Do you have a clear strategy for addressing stealth applicants? How are you engaging students who apply without prior interaction with your institution?

Action Steps

- Conduct a funnel analysis to identify where students are most likely to drop off. Use this data to refine your engagement strategies at each stage.
- Implement personalized inquiry engagement by creating segmented email sequences, hosting targeted events, and using peer-driven social media campaigns to build relationships before pushing applications.
- Develop a professional development plan for your admissions team, ensuring they receive training in relationship-building, long-term follow-up, and student engagement.
- Establish minimum follow-up benchmarks for admissions counselors, ensuring inquiries and applicants receive consistent outreach beyond an initial call.
- Create a summer engagement plan to combat melt, including peer connection programs, student success

spotlights, and digital engagement strategies that keep students excited about attending.

- Implement community-building initiatives during orientation and the first semester to foster belonging and reduce early attrition.
- Use targeted messaging to re-engage stealth applicants, ensuring they feel welcomed and connected to the institution despite not having been in the traditional recruitment funnel.

10

BRAND MARKETING: BE A ZEBRA IN A HERD OF HORSES

"In order to get to the next level of whatever you're doing, you must think and act in a wildly different way than you previously have been."
—Grant Cardone

HIGHER EDUCATION MARKETING is stuck in a time warp. While the rest of the marketing world has embraced data-driven strategies, digital innovation, and audience-first approaches, many institutions are still relying on the same tactics they used decades ago. Today's students aren't flipping through brochures or making decisions based on a generic campus billboard. Yet, instead of adapting, many institutions continue to push outdated strategies, convinced that what worked in the past will work forever. I'm here to tell you: It won't.

One of the biggest challenges is the lack of specialized insight. Too often, institutions lean on partners who don't fully understand the complexity of their audience or the unique decision-making process behind choosing a school.

Higher education isn't a one-size-fits-all industry, and treating it like any other consumer product is a costly mistake. You're not selling sneakers or subscriptions. You're asking people to make one of the most personal, expensive, and life-shaping decisions of their lives. That decision isn't made in a single click or on impulse. It's made over months, sometimes years, often with the input of parents, peers, and financial considerations. That level of nuance requires a different kind of marketing rooted in empathy, trust-building, and long-term engagement.

I recently got off a call with an institution that's in talks with *nine different marketing agencies*. Nine! And out of those nine, maybe three actually understand the nuances of higher ed marketing. Yet, this institution didn't see why choosing an agency that specializes in higher education made a difference. In my opinion, that's like hiring a wedding planner to manage a construction project. Sure, they both require project management skills, but the strategies and end goals are completely different.

Think about how most consumer decisions happen. You realize you need something, maybe a new phone, a pair of running shoes, even just a coffee. You might research a bit, check reviews, compare options, and then make a decision, often within an hour or even a few minutes. The process is relatively quick, driven by immediate needs, convenience, and price.

But no high school junior wakes up one morning and suddenly decides, "I think I'll go to college today." The decision to attend college is an emotional, long-term, high-stakes choice that is about identity, belonging, and envisioning the next chapter of life. Marketing to it like an impulse buy or a short-term purchasing decision completely misunderstands the psychology behind it.

It's time for institutions to stop chasing generic, commercialized marketing tactics. Just because a McDonald's campaign was successful doesn't mean you should copy it. So that brings us to the real question: Where *should* you be looking for inspiration?

PLAYING THE COMPARISON GAME

When searching for inspiration, the first instinct is to look at what other colleges and universities are doing. While that's a logical place to start, the key is looking at the right institutions. If you're a small, private college with a niche student population, comparing yourself to a massive state flagship institution with a *gazillion*-dollar budget is counterproductive.

I see this mistake all the time. A small college will see a campaign from a large public institution and think, "We should be doing something like that!" But marketing is about effectiveness, not imitation. A state flagship institution can afford to take a brute-force brand awareness approach, covering highways with billboards, blanketing digital spaces with ads, and dominating Google search results with paid placements. But it is likely not what your institution needs.

If your goal is to attract mission-fit students who will thrive at your institution, mass exposure isn't the answer. Instead, you need to focus on reaching the students who are actively searching for a place where they belong, a place that aligns with their values, interests, and goals. A hyper-targeted, strategic campaign tailored to your audience will always outperform a scattershot approach trying to reach everyone.

I call this the Goldilocks Effect—not too big, not too small, but just right for your institution's goals, brand, and available resources.

Learn from Corporate Brands

One of the most successful higher ed marketing strategies I've seen recently came from Purdue University. And it was so successful because they stopped looking to other institutions for inspiration.

Purdue is a state flagship institution, so it would have been easy for them to follow the same marketing playbook as every other major public university, including big ad buys, large-scale branding efforts, and prestige-focused messaging. Instead, their approach challenges the assumption that you have to mirror competitors to be successful. It's a reminder that sometimes the better question isn't, "What would our competitor do?" but "What would Red Bull do?" which shifts the focus from conformity to bold, audience-driven creativity.

In previous chapters, we discussed that major consumer brands like Nike, Red Bull, and Apple don't just sell products—they sell identities, aspirations, and emotions. They know that people buy stories first and products second. Red Bull isn't selling energy drinks, they are selling adrenaline and adventure. They make you feel like *you* are part of an extreme, action-packed lifestyle when you purchase their products.

Purdue saw this and decided to apply that same mindset to higher education. Instead of treating marketing as an informational exercise, they shifted to a brand activation approach—which is when your brand stops being a logo and starts feeling like an experience. They studied how other industries create emotional connections and applied those strategies to their own messaging. And that led to one of the most innovative higher education marketing campaigns in recent years.

"Boilers to Mars"

Let's take a closer look at this campaign Purdue put together based on their brand activation approach. Instead of producing yet another facts-and-figures brochure about why their STEM programs are superior, Purdue made a short film.  Not a commercial. Not a recruitment video. A fifteen-minute, Hollywood-level production called "Boilers to Mars." You can scan the QR code to watch it. I recommend you do. It's a tearjerker.

The premise? The first people to set foot on Mars will be Purdue graduates. They created an emotional narrative. One where you see Purdue students discovering and preparing for their upcoming launch. It explores what it means to go to space, including the risks, the hopes, and the race to get there. When watching it, you feel inspired and ready to be a part of something greater. That's powerful. Instead of listing statistics about their aerospace engineering program, they told a story that taps into the core of human ambition.

Let's break down why this works so well:

1. **It creates an emotional hook.** Facts and figures engage the brain, but stories engage the heart. Prospective students watching this are feeling something. They're picturing themselves as future pioneers, not just as students.
2. **It frames Purdue as a launchpad for big dreams.** Purdue could have led with, "We have one of the top aerospace engineering programs in the country." Instead, they framed it in a way that matters to students, stating, "If you want to go to Mars one day, Purdue is the place that will get you there."
3. **It fits with their brand messaging.** "Every Giant Leap Starts with One Small Step" and their brand "The persistent pursuit of the next giant leap."[73]
4. **It's aspirational and inclusive.** You don't have to be an aerospace engineer to feel inspired by this. The message applies to anyone with big dreams. Purdue is telling students, whatever your Mars is, whatever big thing you want to achieve, we can help you get there.
5. **It breaks out of the higher ed mold.** This doesn't look like a traditional higher ed marketing piece. And that's exactly why it works. It stands out in a sea of sameness, where most universities are running variations of the same predictable campaigns.

The takeaway isn't that you need to go out and produce a Hollywood-quality film. It's that you need to start thinking about how to tell stories that resonate emotionally. If you're a small liberal arts college, how do you create a vision where students see themselves growing into leaders, thinkers, and changemakers?

If you're a faith-based institution, how do you make students feel the spiritual and personal transformation they'll experience on your campus?

HIGHER ED NEEDS A NEW PLAYBOOK

In 1998, I was working with Motorola at the same time I was building my first higher education website. Back then, Motorola was at the cutting edge of mobile technology, launching features people had never seen before such as text messaging, picture messaging, and multimedia capabilities. The internet was still new, and the idea that you could take a picture with your phone and send it to someone was revolutionary.

I spent months in their war room, learning how to explain these features to consumers before they even knew they wanted them. Motorola knew exactly who their target audience was: teenagers. They were focused on creating an experience and shaping their messaging around what young people actually cared about.

Then it hit me. These were the same students colleges were trying to recruit. The question wasn't why higher ed wasn't spending millions on research, but why we weren't paying closer attention to the brands that were already investing that money to understand this audience.

At the time, most colleges were still marketing the way they always had—brochures, print ads, and stiff websites filled with academic jargon. Meanwhile, brands like Target, Nike, and Nickelodeon were studying youth culture and shaping their advertising around what actually moved that audience. So, I started watching. I paid attention to how these brands crafted messaging that resonated emotionally, and how they built experiences that pulled their audience (like my own children) in.

The problem with higher education marketing is that it's insular. Institutions tend to recycle ideas rather than innovate, looking at what peer institutions are doing instead of considering how to truly capture attention. Ideas circulate, get repackaged, and resurface in slightly different forms. But if all you're doing is pulling from the same well, you're not going to get anything new.

This is one of the most self-referential industries out there. Colleges benchmark against other colleges. They analyze competitors and tweak their strategies, but rarely do they step outside the academic bubble to see how global brands are engaging audiences.

Meanwhile, students aren't just seeing marketing from other institutions, they're seeing marketing *everywhere*. Their world is filled with ads from brands that know how to engage, inspire, and activate their audience. If your messaging looks and sounds the same as every other institution, it gets lost in the noise.

Instead of asking how other colleges are promoting themselves, institutions should be asking: How do major brands with massive consumer engagement capture attention? What strategies are brands spending millions of dollars of research on that seem to be working? Major brands are footing the bill for the research—higher ed just needs to apply the lessons. All you have to do is pay attention to the strategies that work and find ways to bring them into your higher education marketing.

REVERSE-ENGINEERING GREAT MARKETING

Every time you come across an ad, a website, or a campaign that catches your eye, you need to put on your journalist's hat. Go back to seventh grade and apply the fundamental questions of storytelling: Who, What, When, Where, Why, and How.

When we see a campaign that stands out, it's easy to get excited and think, "We should try something like this!" That spark of inspiration is valuable, but the next step should be thoughtful analysis instead of replication. What exactly made the campaign effective? Why did it grab attention? And most importantly, would it speak to your audience in the same way? Taking time to unpack the strategy behind the idea can turn admiration into meaningful action.

Let's start with who. Who is the ad designed for? If you're a fifty-five-year-old college administrator, and you see an ad that resonates with you, that doesn't necessarily mean it will resonate with a seventeen-year-old high school student. We all have personal preferences, but those preferences are shaped by our experiences, our generation, and the media we consume. The question isn't, do *I* like this? The question is, would my target audience like this? If it's an ad for a brand targeting Gen Z, study it. If it's geared toward middle-aged professionals, set it aside—unless your campaign is aimed at adult learners or other non-traditional audiences, in which case the context changes everything!

Next, ask what. What is this ad trying to communicate? Every well-crafted ad has a purpose. It's either telling a story, triggering an emotional response, or driving a specific action. Is it trying to sell a product? Is it trying to associate a brand with a lifestyle? Is it creating urgency? Look at the call to action. Is it asking you to buy, to sign up, to share, or just to remember the brand? Before you can apply any lessons to your own marketing, you need to fully grasp the intended goal of the original piece.

Now, consider when it's being shown. Timing plays a crucial role in advertising. Different audiences are engaged at different times. If you're watching a football game, the majority of ads are tailored to a male audience, although, thanks to Taylor Swift and the Swiftie effect at Kansas City Chiefs games, we're seeing a shift in demographics. The key takeaway? Think about when your audience is most receptive. When do high school students start seriously thinking about college? When do parents get involved in decision-making? What time of the day are they consuming media? If you can align your marketing efforts with the natural decision-making timeline, your message will land more effectively.

Then, ask where. Where is this ad being placed? A brilliantly crafted ad might not be effective if it's in the wrong location. A billboard, a YouTube pre-roll, a TikTok ad, a Spotify sponsorship—each platform has a different audience and a different level of engagement. If you're advertising on radio, for example, you need to consider the kind of audience that still listens to radio. If you're running digital ads, you need to be strategic about the platforms your audience is using. A beautifully produced 60-second TV spot might be irrelevant if your audience spends most of their time on social media. Placement matters just as much as messaging.

The next question is why. Why is this ad effective? Why does it make people feel a certain way? Why does it stick? Great marketing moves people. It sparks something inside them. Sometimes it's humor, sometimes it's nostalgia, sometimes it's pure aspiration. Every memorable ad has an emotional core. When you break down an ad, pay attention to how it makes you feel, and more importantly, why it makes you feel that way. That's where the real magic happens.

Finally, the most important question. How can you take inspiration from this ad and apply it to your institution without copying it outright? How can you achieve the same emotional impact without spending millions on production? The goal isn't to replicate, it's to adapt. Maybe a brand uses storytelling to highlight customer transformation, so, you ask yourself how you can use storytelling to showcase the transformation your students experience? Maybe a company uses humor to break through the noise. How can you infuse personality into your marketing to feel more human?

Great marketers, like great artists, know how to borrow wisely. They don't plagiarize, they observe, remix, and reimagine. They find inspiration in unexpected places and transform it into something that feels fresh and authentic to their brand. The result is innovation built on insight.

If you train yourself to look at marketing through a journalistic lens, you'll start to see opportunities everywhere. The best part? You won't need a billion-dollar ad budget to test and research so you can create something powerful. You'll just need to pay attention to the brands who have the same audience as you.

WHAT DOES IT MEAN TO BE A ZEBRA?

One of the biggest mistakes institutions make in marketing is trying to appeal to everyone. They worry that if they lean too hard into their distinctiveness, they will alienate potential students. So, they water down their messaging, trying to be broad, neutral, and universally appealing. The result is a brand that's forgettable.

General marketing doesn't inspire students to enroll. Students enroll because the institution feels right for them. That only happens when an institution embraces its true identity, even if it means not being the perfect fit for everyone.

The best brands in the world aren't afraid to be bold in their positioning. They don't try to be liked by everyone. They create such a strong identity that their ideal customers feel an immediate connection, and those who don't are filtered out before they make it further along the funnel. Higher ed institutions need to take the same approach.

In medicine, there's a common saying, "When you hear hoofbeats, think horses, not zebras." Doctors are trained to diagnose based on the most likely explanation. If a patient comes in with a cough and fever, they probably have the flu, not some rare, exotic disease. Medical professionals are taught to look for the obvious answer first, because nine times out of ten, that's what it is.

But when it comes to marketing higher education, the exact opposite is true. If you're at a college fair, lined up alongside thirty other institutions, all handing out brochures and saying essentially the same thing, why would a student remember you? If all they see is a herd of identical horses, how do they make a decision? They don't. They collect information, nod politely, and forget about your institution as soon as they walk away.

That's why you need to be the zebra among a herd of horses and let your stripes set you apart. You don't have to be the loudest or the flashiest, but letting your uniqueness stand on its own will make your institution memorable.

Now, let me be clear: Standing out isn't about being different just for the sake of it. It's not about wearing a neon green suit to a recruitment event or having a viral social media challenge if it has nothing to do with your institution's identity. It's about being different in a way that is authentic to your institution.

Think about your messaging. If you're saying the same things as every other institution (small class sizes, close-knit community, strong academic programs) then you're just another horse in the herd. None of those things are bad, but they also aren't differentiators. If a student can't tell what makes you unique, they won't feel a strong pull toward your institution.[74]

Now, imagine a student walking through a college fair, overwhelmed by the sea of sameness. Then, they come across an institution that owns its identity. Maybe it's an institution that leans fully into its quirky and creative culture. Maybe it's a faith-based institution that doesn't just mention its values but actively shows how those values shape the student experience. Maybe it's a STEM-heavy institution that frames itself not as "offering great engineering programs" but as "producing the next pioneers in space exploration." That's a zebra moment.

So, ask yourself:

What is the one thing your institution does better than anyone else?

- What kind of student would thrive in your environment?
- What values define your institution's culture, and are you clearly communicating them?
- If you took your logo off your website, would your messaging still feel distinct? Or could it belong to any other college?

The institutions that win in marketing aren't necessarily the biggest, the richest, or even the most prestigious. But they are the ones that own their identity with confidence.

TAKE ACTION

It's easy to get caught in the routine of doing what's always been done. But standing out in higher education marketing requires intention, not just chasing trends. The following exercises and reflection points are designed to help you apply the ideas from this chapter to your unique context. Take time to work through them, either on your own or with your team, and use them as a springboard for meaningful conversations and actionable insights.

Reflective Questions

- Is there a better way of doing what we are doing? If we weren't constrained by "the way it's always been done," how would we approach this differently?
- Are we missing an example of what we want to achieve? Have we looked outside of higher ed for inspiration? What industries could we be learning from?
- Where did this idea come from? If the answer is, "Our competitors do it," stop and reconsider. Are we doing something because it's effective—or because we're following the herd?
- Are we being different for difference's sake? Does our approach clarify who we are, or are we just chasing attention? Shock value alone isn't a strategy—our distinctiveness should reinforce our identity.

Action Steps

- Review your website, brochures, ads, and recruitment materials. If you swapped out your institution's name and logo with a competitor's, would it still feel unique to you? If not, it's time to refine your messaging.
- Assign your team to research consumer brands that connect well with younger audiences—Nike, Apple, Red Bull, Target. Host a brainstorming session where you analyze what makes these brands stand out and discuss how similar storytelling and engagement strategies could apply to your institution.
- Ask your team, "What is something we do better than anyone else?" Clarify your institution's unique value proposition in a way that is compelling to your audience.
- Conduct informal student focus groups or surveys to see what resonates. Experiment with small-scale campaigns that lean into a distinct message, then track engagement and response.
- Encourage your marketing team to reverse-engineer successful ads using the "Who, What, When, Where, Why, and How" method. Discuss your findings and how you can apply these new strategies to your ads moving forward.
- Commit to one bold change in your marketing approach—whether it's shifting your storytelling strategy, rethinking your visuals, or refining how you communicate your value. Don't be afraid to lean into what makes you you. The institutions that stand out are the ones that own their identity with confidence.

11

MARKETING THROUGH LEADERSHIP: THINK LIKE A CEO

"Times are tough so we cut marketing, ensuring that times will get tougher."
—Jeff Spear, Founder and President of CFO College

HIGHER ED LEADERSHIP carry a lot of weight on their shoulders. Presidents, the board, and cabinet leaders are tasked with honoring legacy, protecting mission, supporting students, and stewarding the future, all while managing limited resources in an increasingly unpredictable landscape. It's not an easy job. And for many years, the challenges were steady but manageable. Institutions followed familiar rhythms, enrollment was relatively predictable, and the decisions often felt rooted in tradition. But the ground has shifted.

Now, declining demographics, changing student expectations, and increased competition are forcing higher ed institutions to think differently. Don't look at this as a bad thing;
look at it as an opportunity. Now more than ever, institutional
leaders have the chance to bring in a new kind of thinking. The
kind aligns people, programs, and priorities to ensure long-term
sustainability for their institution. In other words: it's time to
think like a CEO.

Now, I'm not advocating you should turn your campus into
a corporation. Academic tradition matters. But we want our
missions to thrive for the long haul. Thinking like a CEO means
asking better questions. It means being proactive, instead of
reactive. It means building systems that serve students, not just
processes that work for staff. And most importantly, it means
making sure the impact of your institution can continue, for this
generation and the next.

This chapter is about stepping into that mindset. I won't ask
you to give up on what makes higher education unique, but there
are three key areas you can strengthen your processes by looking
at them through a lens of the CEO. They include Marketing,
Sales, and Customer Service. Let's take a closer look at each.

MARKETING THROUGH THE LENS OF A CEO

In higher ed, we talk a lot about cost. But when it comes to
marketing, I want to reframe the conversation. Because this isn't
about cost, it's about return on investment.

The trouble is that marketing is still treated like a support
service. Historically, communications in higher ed grew out of
supporting advancement, handling things like donor newsletters,

event announcements, and press releases. Like food services or landscaping, it was seen as something nice to have, but easy to cut when budgets got tight. What's often missed is that if it's done right, marketing isn't a cost center at all, it's an investment strategy.

Most institutions would never think of cutting their advancement department because they see it as a revenue stream. They understand the role it plays in donor relations and long-term funding. But marketing? That's often the first thing on the chopping block. It's not seen as a driver of revenue, and that mindset is costing institutions dearly.

If you do marketing right, it becomes the engine that drives tuition revenue. It's what connects you to your mission-fit students, and it's what keeps enrollment sustainable.

Look at the hospitality industry. Hotels and airlines don't just run on great service. They rely heavily on brand perception and customer experience. When they start cutting corners in the name of efficiency, they often lose the very thing that made them successful in the first place. Just look at Southwest Airlines. For years, they built a strong, distinctive brand around simplicity, friendliness, and customer-first perks like free checked bags and no change fees. But recently, they've begun shifting that model, reducing or removing many of the very elements that set them apart. In doing so, they have put their brand loyalty at risk.

It's a cautionary tale. Once you start abandoning what made you different (in higher education's case, this comes from cutting your marketing budget), you become just another option in an already crowded space. One of the best examples of this comes from outside our industry.

In 1985, Coca-Cola made an attempt to compete with Pepsi's sweeter taste by reformulating their classic product. They called it "New Coke."[75] But what they thought was a savvy competitive play turned out to be a disaster. Loyal customers were outraged. They didn't want a sweeter Coke. They wanted the original. The backlash was so intense that Coke had to backpedal within months and bring back the original formula rebranded as "Coca-Cola Classic."

The customer backlash came from more than the change in taste. It was about identity. Coca-Cola underestimated how emotionally attached people were to the original product. That red can represented more than a beverage. For their customers, it stood for nostalgia, tradition, and familiarity. By trying to chase a trend, they alienated the very people who had built the brand's legacy. The lesson? When you lose sight of what your audience values most, even a well-intentioned strategy can backfire.

Higher ed institutions make the same mistake when they chase trends or slash budgets without thinking about long-term brand impact. Or worse, when they let the loudest internal voice in the room dictate direction even when that voice doesn't represent their mission-fit student.

As a leader, you'll face several layers of pressure. Internal stakeholders, board members, donors, and faculty will all have opinions about what should be done, what should be cut, what "used to work." But your job isn't to please the loudest person in the meeting. Your job is to make decisions based on data, alignment, and the needs of your mission-fit student. Incorporating a P&L—a profit and loss statement that shows the revenues generated and expenses incurred for a specific area—into your marketing can help with these decisions by making the financial impact clear and measurable.

Yes, Marketing Needs Its Own P&L

Higher ed has a complicated relationship with the idea of profit. Talk to most institutional leaders about a profit and loss statement (P&L), and you'll likely get a wary look. Many institutions hesitate to view themselves as businesses. They bristle at the language of revenue, ROI, or market share. After all, education is a mission. It's about transformations, not transactions.

I agree with that, to a point. But if your institution can't sustain itself financially, the mission doesn't matter because eventually the doors will close. You can't fulfill your purpose if you're underwater. Which is why it's time to borrow a page from the business world and start applying a CEO mindset to your institution's operations, especially when it comes to your academic programs and your marketing efforts.

On our podcast, *The Higher Ed Marketer*,[76] we recently sat down with Eric Hogue, President of Colorado Christian University, and he told us that *every academic program at CCU is required to submit a P&L statement each year*. He said, "I looked at each division as a division in the company...each division has to be profitable within itself...otherwise it is not sustainable." This means the institution doesn't assume a program is worth keeping because it's been around for a while or because a few passionate faculty members want to fight for it. They look at the numbers and ask if it's bringing in enough revenue to cover its costs.

If not? It's either time to market it differently or time to sunset the program. That might sound harsh, but it's not. It's healthy. It's objective. And it's the kind of strategic clarity more institutions need if they want to survive the enrollment cliff.

The reality is a lot of institutions are subsidizing programs that only serve three or four students. But when you factor in the cost of faculty, classroom space, office resources, and administrative support, you're losing money on that program every single year. In any other industry, that would be a red flag. It would get shut down, or at the very least, restructured. But in higher ed? We keep it alive out of tradition.

If you're running marketing correctly, meaning you've done the market research and you understand your mission-fit student, then you'll know whether a program has real potential or not. If it doesn't, you need to be honest about it. And you need the data to back that up, which the P&L will give you.

Too often, marketing gets blamed when a program fails. The department says, "We're not getting enough students." Admissions says, "There's no demand for this degree." Both sides point fingers at the marketing created for it. But a proper P&L helps everyone align around the facts. It brings clarity. It empowers you to either invest in growing the program or sunset it. That same logic applies to marketing itself.

Marketing is not just another expense line on your budget spreadsheet. Or at least, it shouldn't be. If you're doing it right, marketing is an investment, one that pays back in the form of increased enrollment, improved yield, and long-term revenue growth.

Some institutions are beginning to shift their mindset. When the budget gets tight, they don't treat marketing as an expense to be cut, they treat it as an investment that needs to be protected. I've worked with institutions that have pursued bank loans specifically to fund their enrollment marketing efforts. Others have launched donor-driven campaigns to get the money for brand visibility campaigns, digital campaigns, and marketing technology upgrades. It's a smart move. After all, you can raise millions to build a state-of-the-art residence hall, but if enrollment keeps dropping, who's going to live in it? In times of decline or transition, it's marketing that often holds the key to recovery.

SALES

Your enrollment team is your sales team. You can have the best marketing strategy in the world, but if your enrollment team isn't ready to convert leads, it's all for nothing.

Too many times, we have been brought in to help an institution generate more leads, only to get stalled by an enrollment department who doesn't know how to sell. We refine the message. We clean up the website. We launch targeted campaigns. And the leads start coming in. But then? Nothing happens. The handoff from marketing to enrollment falls flat. The enrollment team doesn't have processes for follow-up or relationship building. There is no intentional sales process for them to follow. You can almost hear the sound of opportunity walking out the door.

Marketing and enrollment don't always speak the same language, but they are part of the same system. If you're investing in marketing without investing in your sales process, you're just driving traffic into an empty room.

Worse, your marketing ends up getting blamed because there was no system in place to convert the interest it generated. What's more, higher ed isn't known for having world-class sales training. In many institutions, you have a twenty-two-year-old counselor, fresh out of college themselves, managing a conversation that could change someone's life…and nobody has given them the tools to handle it well. That's not a marketing failure. That's a system failure.

To fix it, you need to look at the entire house, not just the roof. Is your enrollment team trained in relationship selling? Are they responsive? Do they understand how to build trust over time? Are you optimizing the full enrollment funnel, not just the top? If not, your institution will miss out on key moments to connect with your mission-fit students.

I recently had Jay Baer on the *Higher Ed Marketer* podcast.[77] He and I discussed the topic of "speed to lead" and how it's become non-negotiable in today's instant-gratification world.[78] Jay shared how fast response time can make or break a conversion. People don't want to wait. They don't want a brochure in the mail next week. They want answers right now.

Grand Canyon University and University of Phoenix have taken this seriously. They pride themselves on speed. When a student fills out a form, they call within sixty seconds, day or night. Now compare that to most traditional institutions where it might take a week before someone gets a response. A week! In that time, your prospect has probably heard from three other institutions...or changed their mind entirely.

Responding slowly isn't an option anymore. Our enrollment departments need faster response times, multiple communication channels, and nurturing campaigns that don't rely on a single email or voicemail. You can't treat prospective students like they are the ones who need to conform to your process. You need to meet them where they are.

Think about your own life. I recently spent two months playing voicemail tag with a doctor's office just to schedule an appointment. They refused to confirm by voicemail, email, or texting as I preferred, and I couldn't call during their narrow office hours. Eventually they just stopped calling. That's not customer service. That's an inconvenience wrapped in process.

Now imagine your prospective student going through the same thing, calling during their lunch break, getting no answer, waiting days for a reply, then being expected to take a call at ten a.m. on a weekday while they are at school. It's no wonder they disappear. We are creating more friction for them!

We have to flip the script. What if your enrollment team shifted their workday to make calls after three p.m. when high school students are actually available? What if you prioritized texting or live chat because your audience prefers it? What if you stopped thinking like an institution and started thinking like your user?

This is how we reduce friction and meet our mission-fit students where they are. If we keep designing processes that work well for us, but not for them, they'll go somewhere else. And then, it won't matter how good your marketing is.

CUSTOMER SERVICE

If you're concerned about enrollment, you should be just as concerned about retention. I not enough to get students in the door—you also have to keep them.

National data tells us that only 68.2% of first-year students return for their sophomore year. That means nearly a third of students don't come back after just one year. By the time you stretch out the window to six years—the most common graduation tracking timeline—only 62.2% of students earn their degree.[79]

That's a lot of effort and budget going into students who never cross the finish line. And let's not forget this varies by institution. Community colleges retain just over half of their first-year students. Even private four-year institutions, with all their personalized opportunities, still lose nearly a quarter of their first-year class.

We're working so hard to recruit students, to get them excited, to push applications, to fill out FAFSA, to submit their deposit. But once they commit, once they move in, we stop wooing them. The honeymoon's over. We treat students like VIPs until they enroll. Then we go quiet for four years. That is, until they graduate, and suddenly we're calling again. This time, for money.

How would you feel as a student if this was the interaction your institution had with you? They push and push to get you there, go radio silent once you step foot on campus, then start calling for money once you leave? Would that make you want to donate? Would it make you feel like your institution cares?

Retention is a customer service issue *and* a marketing opportunity. Every time a student goes home for fall break, winter break, or summer, there's an opportunity for them not to come back. Life happens. They get distracted, discouraged, and disillusioned. Unless we're actively showing them why they belong, and what a difference your institution can make in their lives, they'll drift.

This is where human-centered campaigns can make students feel seen, valued, and supported. Western Governors University has modeled this well in recent advertising. Their campaign speaks directly to prospective students who've been told that college is too expensive, too time-consuming, or out of reach unless they quit their jobs or upend their lives. WGU flips that narrative by showing students that there is a path forward that fits their reality. The message is simple but powerful: *We know what you've heard, and we've built something different because we believe you deserve access.* That kind of empathetic messaging attracts students and retains them because it reinforces that this institution understands and supports their journey.

But retention can't start and stop with marketing. It requires a campus-wide mindset. Every corner of the institution should be attuned to signs of disengagement and ready to step in with care.

This is where institutions should be operating like a five-star hotel. Think about it. When you walk into a good hotel, they don't just hand you a key and walk away. They ask how your trip was. Offer a bottle of water. Tell you where to find breakfast. Every touchpoint says, "We see you. We're glad you're here." Will Guidara's book *Unreasonable Hospitality*,[80] unpacks this mindset in detail, showing how small, intentional gestures can create unforgettable experiences that turn customers into loyal advocates.

Higher ed is a highly competitive marketplace. Not just with other institutions, but with *life*. Financial pressure. Family needs. Mental health. All these nuances are pulling at the students in your institution. It's not always another college that steals our students—it's stress, or burnout, or just a sense that nobody cares if they stay.

The attrition rate for undergrads is close to 33%, and among first-year students, it's over 24%.[81] To me, that's a flashing red light for institutions who are focused solely on recruitment without a solid retention strategy. So, what does real student-centered service look like?

I'll give you a small but powerful example. Dr. Nido Qubein, president of High Point University,[82] was on my podcast not long ago. Around Thanksgiving, I saw something on their Instagram that blew me away.[83] Right before the holiday break, they offer free car checkups for students heading home. They hire mechanics to check oil, tire pressure, and basic maintenance to make sure students are safe on the road. Students line up to have their car looked at, and the president walks among them, greeting them, talking to them, and asking them to travel safely as they go home. Think about what that signals, not just to the student, but to their parents. This institution doesn't just want your tuition. They want you whole, healthy, and safe. That's care that will create retention.

Every time a student leaves, it costs the institution thousands, sometimes tens of thousands, in lost revenue. So why wouldn't we invest in the small things that keep our mission-fit students feeling connected?

We can't ignore the melt either, the moment when students say "yes," but never show up. They fill out their paperwork, they pick their dorm, they register for classes... and then they vanish. That melt rate can be 10% or more, and when your entire enrollment strategy is based on forecasting tuition revenue, that kind of drop-off can wreck your financial model.

Often, the breakdown here happens at the handoff from admissions to student life. It's like a baton pass in a relay race. If it's fumbled, the momentum is lost. If it's smooth and student-focused, the race continues. Orientation and registration are high-risk touchpoints. They should be designed not just to "get students settled" but to reinforce their decision to come in the first place and why they belong at your institution. That's where the relationship needs to *deepen*, not go silent.

So, ask yourself:

- How are we checking in with students emotionally, not just academically?
- What kind of follow-up do we have after the first week, the first month, the first break?
- How are we making it easier for students to stay than to leave?

If you're serious about retention, then you're serious about customer service. And if you're serious about customer service, then marketing is never really done.

IT'S TIME TO THINK LIKE A BUSINESS

At some point, institutional leadership has to make a decision. Are we going to keep thinking like an academic institution alone, or are we going to start thinking like a business too?

For decades, higher ed didn't have to compete like other industries. In fact, until about twenty years ago, college admissions felt a lot like holding out a catcher's mitt. You just opened enrollment season, held out your glove, and a steady stream of students landed inside. If you were a faith-based institution, you could count on a consistent pipeline from church communities. If you were a local community college, you knew you'd enroll a reliable number of high school graduates from nearby districts. Enrollment was stable. Predictable. Almost automatic.

But that world is gone. The enrollment cliff has changed everything. And it's not just a demographic issue, but a cultural one. Students now see many different paths to success. Trades are being promoted heavily (and rightly so). Young people are doing the math and realizing they can enter the workforce without accruing massive debt. Apprenticeships, certifications, bootcamps, and masterclasses offer more ways than ever to launch a career that does not involve a four-year degree. If your institution is only selling career readiness, you're going to struggle. This is the moment to pivot, from career readiness to life readiness.

The value of college isn't just the diploma. It's the mindset, the critical thinking, the relationships, the experience of learning how to live and grow with other people. That's what stuck with me most from my own college experience. I have a degree in graphic design, but I don't work as a graphic designer. What I *do* carry with me every day are the problem-solving skills, the resilience, and the ways of thinking I picked up during those four years. That's what we should be marketing. That's what we should be designing for. And that's what we should be protecting as leaders.

In a saturated marketplace with fewer students and more choices, relevance is everything. If you're not clearly communicating why it still deserves a place in someone's life journey, you will lose ground.

TAKE ACTION

Thinking like a CEO gives institutional leadership a new way to evaluate risk, allocate resources strategically, and focus on long-term sustainability. The following exercises and reflection points are designed to help you apply the ideas from this chapter to your unique context. Take time to work through them, either on your own or with your team, and use them as a springboard for meaningful conversations and actionable insights.

Reflective Questions

- Are we treating marketing as a cost or as a revenue-driving investment?
- Do we have clear data to show which academic programs are profitable and which are not?
- When a prospective student inquires, how fast do we respond, and through what channels?
- How aligned are our marketing, admissions, and student life teams? Where are the handoffs breaking down?
- What do our current students hear from us between move-in and graduation? Are we still wooing them?
- Are we preparing students for a job or preparing them for life?
- What traditions or assumptions are we clinging to that no longer serve our students or our sustainability?

Action Steps

- Sit down with your CFO or VP of Marketing and create a marketing P&L. Map out what you're spending on marketing and what you're getting back in terms of inquiries, conversions, and tuition revenue. Look at it like an investor would.
- Require each academic program to create an annual P&L statement. Measure not just enrollment but cost of delivery, market demand, and long-term viability.
- Outline exactly what happens from the moment a prospective student fills out a form. Define timelines, roles, response standards, and escalation points. Your enrollment funnel shouldn't have leaks.
- Identify key moments when students are most at risk of leaving (after midterms, before breaks, during registration) and design outreach, events, and campaigns to keep students engaged and connected.
- Invest in sales training for your enrollment team—not just customer service scripts, but coaching on empathy, objections, follow-ups, and value-based conversations. Help them build trust, not just answer questions.
- Bring together departments for a cross-functional meeting focused on retention. Ask: "What would five-star service look like at our institution?" Then take one idea and pilot it next semester.

12

DATA DRIVEN MARKETING: THE RISE OF THE CO-BOTS

"Data is the sword of the 21st century, those who wield it well, the samurai."

— Jonathan Rosenberg

IF YOU'VE WORKED in higher education long enough, you've probably seen the evolution of data systems firsthand, or at least heard stories about it. Back in the 1970s, data lived on magnetic tape. Reports were generated through punch cards and mainframes, and the only people who could make sense of it were computer engineers or trained data scientists.

Enrollment data was managed on index cards, often filed away in physical boxes that admissions officers would sort through manually. Alumni data lived somewhere else. Prospective student data (if it was collected at all) was rarely connected to anything beyond basic outreach. The registrar's office was often the only place where data was structured in a usable system.

Fast forward a few decades, and although most institutions have traded paper for digital tools, the problem hasn't gone away, it's just become more complicated. I recently spoke with a leader in ed tech who estimated that the average institution has between two hundred and three hundred different databases, and most of them don't talk to each other!

That's hundreds of sources of information, each sitting in its own silo. Enrollment, advancement, marketing, student success, finance, all pulling data from separate systems, with limited visibility across departments. And when your data is fragmented, your strategy is too. Important insights are lost, patterns are missed, and decisions are delayed.

Historically, if you wanted to get a clear picture of your data, you had to know exactly what you were looking for. Then you'd need someone with the skills to write a SQL query, generate a report, export it, and manually reformat the results. Because most answers led to new questions, the process often took weeks to get a full picture, by which time, the data was likely no longer relevant. Luckily, that is no longer the case.

I often hear from institutions that they struggle with limited data, especially when it comes to things like email addresses or student contact information. While that can be a real hurdle, it often signals something deeper. Sometimes we miss opportunities to uncover the insights already at our fingertips. It's not always about needing more data. It's about making better use of the data we already have. In many cases, the solution isn't more collection, but smarter collaboration, cleaner systems, and stronger follow-through.

In today's world, privacy (as we used to define it) no longer really exists. Companies like Google, Meta, and Amazon already have a digital profile of who you are, what you want, and what you're likely to do next. The marketing teams behind major retailers aren't guessing. They're watching buying patterns, connecting dots, and using algorithms making predictions for what you'll buy next based on your behavior. And they've been doing it for years.

One of the most well-known stories of predictive data use comes from *The Power of Habit*[84] by Charles Duhigg. In it, he shares a story about a man who walked into a Target store furious because his teenage daughter had received coupons for maternity clothes. He thought Target had crossed a line and couldn't believe they'd assume his teenage daughter would need such things. What he didn't know was that his daughter had already bought a pregnancy test and prenatal vitamins. Target's algorithms had only picked up on those purchases and offered her coupons for other maternity products.

That story might sound unsettling, but it points to a truth higher ed can't afford to ignore: your prospective students, current students, and alumni are leaving digital breadcrumbs everywhere. Corporations are using them to deliver highly per-sonalized, relevant outreach. Why aren't we?

The good news is the same tools are available to you. There are services that can enrich your existing data, help you fill in missing contact details, and create more complete profiles of your audiences. It's called data augmentation, and it's no longer limited to big corporations with massive budgets. If Target can figure out a major life event from a few clicks, surely we can find out whether a student is ready for a transfer conversation or if an alum might be open to re-engaging.

Taking advantage of this data is a mindset shift for much of higher education. But it allows you to become more relevant to your mission-fit student. The people you're trying to reach are already receiving personalized, timely communication from every other part of their lives. If your messages feel out of sync or poorly timed, they'll tune you out. But if you can show up with the right message at the right time? That's when trust starts to build.

Higher ed has a powerful opportunity here. We just need to engage with our data in a more intelligent way. We are living in a time where higher education is *data rich* but *insight poor*. The good news is we have the power to change that.

We don't have the money for integrated systems that large corporations like Target or Walmart have. We also don't have the staff bandwidth to run daily queries or support multiple stakeholders at once. But technology is finally catching up to our needs at a price point institutions can meet.

Today, there are tools (many of them powered by AI) that are helping institutions move from linear, code-based reporting models to conversational, real-time analysis. These tools are designed to work with you, not just for you. They help you ask better questions, access faster insights, and get clear on what's really happening across your institution. They function less like old-school software, and more like collaborative partners. This is where I'm going to bring us back to generative artificial intelligence.

DON'T PROGRAM THE TOOL—PARTNER WITH IT

We're entering a new era of data engagement, one where you don't need to speak fluent SQL or wait three weeks for a report just to answer a basic enrollment question. Thanks to the rise of generative AI, institutions now have the ability to talk to their data instead of playing a long game of telephone between departments, systems, and staff.

This is a fundamental shift because the speed of decision-making matters. In enrollment, advancement, and beyond, the speed of business is the speed to lead. If we can't make decisions quickly based on the right data, we risk losing time *and* opportunity.

The challenge is that many leaders still think of these new AI tools the way we think of traditional software like Microsoft Office. In other words, we assume we have to use the right format, click the right buttons, or type in the exact phrase to get what we want. But that's not how these tools are designed to work. They're not just programs, they're collaborators.

Think of them more like an intern or a new team member. You don't hand an intern a sixty-page manual and expect them to instantly produce a perfect report. Instead, you have a conversation. You explain the goal, set expectations, and give them space to figure out how to get there. The same is true with generative AI. You don't need to write perfect instructions; you need to articulate the outcome you want.

That's a major mindset shift for many leaders, especially those used to systems that demand technical precision. But it's also where the real opportunity lies. Once you start thinking of these tools as intelligent assistants, you unlock a whole new level of efficiency and insight.

And yes, let's be honest, this chapter might feel outdated the minute it's published. These tools are evolving that fast. But that's not a reason to wait. It's a reason to engage now, to start learning the language of AI-assisted leadership, and to build internal habits that help you move with the speed and clarity that today's environment demands.

QUESTIONS OVER COMMANDS

Having the tools to generate reports, build models, or summarize trends is important, but it's not enough. The real value lies in the ability to frame a problem well. To ask the kind of question that opens new insights, sharpens focus, and drives strategy forward. That's a skill rooted in subject matter expertise, not software. It's why the most effective use of AI will always require subject matter expertise.

This is where your institutional knowledge becomes a premium asset. The more you understand your environment, including your mission-fit student, your workflows, and your goals, the more clearly you can articulate what needs to be achieved. That clarity is what makes tools like AI truly useful. Without it, even the most advanced system will spin its wheels. With it, you can make significant progress in a fraction of the time.

While technology keeps evolving, the real game-changer is still our ability to express what we're trying to achieve.

Expressing what's in your head clearly, concisely, and in context, is becoming one of the most important leadership skills of our time. Whether you're giving direction to an AI agent or to a human teammate, your ability to define the goal and outline the parameters will directly affect the quality of the outcomes.

In this way, the tools don't replace the need for human insight, they amplify it. The agents will do the chores. But we're the ones responsible for identifying what needs to be done in the first place. That's a shift from execution to vision. From task management to problem definition. And it's where liberal arts education (learning how to think, communicate, and connect ideas) starts to show its value in a digital world.

Machines can process data, automate outreach, and surface trends, but they can't determine what matters most to your institution, your students, or your mission. That responsibility still falls to human judgment. It's not about handing over decision-making to algorithms. It's about using those tools to extend your capacity so you can focus on the higher-order work: setting direction, aligning stakeholders, and navigating complexity.

We don't need ego-driven leaders who pretend to have every solution, nor do we need leaders who disengage because they feel out of their depth. What we need are leaders who are willing to think critically, ask better questions, and model that behavior for their teams.

One of the best examples I've seen of this in action is Paul Mauer, President at Montreat College in North Carolina. I first connected with his VP of Enrollment at a conference and later had the opportunity to speak at one of their leadership retreats. After the presentation on AI in higher ed, Paul and his team stayed back for a forty-minute conversation and walked away with thirty-five specific action items for how their institution could begin leveraging AI to improve student experience and increase operational efficiency.

Paul didn't walk in with all the answers. He didn't claim to be an AI expert. But he knew enough to ask thoughtful, targeted questions. He was engaged, open-minded, and curious. That mindset helped his team move quickly from theory to application. By the end of the same day, they had already identified and tested an AI tool to support outbound phone calls.

That's what great leadership looks like today. Not being the smartest person in the room but being the most *willing* to learn. Paul understood that asking the right questions was the key to reducing risk, exploring new opportunities, and moving his institution forward.

When you lead with humility and curiosity, you invite smarter systems, and smarter people, into the process. These tools may be more advanced than we are in some areas, but they are designed to *support* us, not replace us. The question is, are we willing to partner with them?

When good questions become the currency of progress, it's not the technologist who leads. It's the strategic thinker. The communicator. The educator who knows how to translate complex goals into focused direction. This is the kind of leadership higher ed will need to thrive in the era that comes next.

REMEMBER THE JOURNALIST METHOD

In the last chapter, I explained what it looks like to analyze the marketing of corporations like a journalist so you could leverage what works into promoting your institution by using the classic six—who, what, when, where, why, and how—questions. But another place you can leverage this thinking is with new technologies.

These questions are the foundation of effective prompts, smart analysis, and strong leadership decisions. If you're trying to understand a dip in enrollment, for example, don't just ask AI for a report. Investigate it like a story.

- Who is impacted? Maybe it's first-generation students.
- What is happening? Their enrollment is down.
- Why? That's the insight you're after, and what's causing the drop?
- Where? Perhaps you're not reaching them in the right geographic areas or digital spaces. List out the spaces you are currently trying to reach them to give context to the AI.
- How? Detail how they're encountering your brand, navigating your website, or receiving communications. Ask AI what's causing friction.

Once you have a potential answer, run those questions again, this time through the lens of what the data reveals. Think of it like building a decision tree, each layer of insight leads to another, helping you move deeper into root causes and more targeted solutions. And with AI-powered tools, you can move through this process faster and more thoroughly than ever before.

This way of approaching a problem with technology encourages curiosity, critical thinking, and proactive leadership. When you engage with AI this way, you stop treating it like a static report creator and start using it as a dynamic problem-solving partner.

FAIL FORWARD

One of the biggest obstacles to using new AI-driven tools is our own expectation of perfection. Too often, we try a tool once, don't get the exact output we were hoping for, and immediately decide it doesn't work. We give up too early, frustrated that the system didn't instantly read our mind or solve our problem on the first try.

But when you add a new hire to your team, you don't expect flawless work on day one. You provide context, guidance, and feedback, and you give them time to learn the nuances of your brand. If they misunderstand a request, you reframe it and give them another shot. That is how we develop people, and it should be how we approach these new tools.

Generative AI and advanced data platforms require a collaborative mindset. They don't "fail" so much as require refinement. If a report doesn't come out the way you expected, or an insight feels off-base, that's not the end of the process, it's the beginning of a conversation. You need to be willing to clarify the goal, provide more context, and adjust the parameters. Every iteration will bring you closer to what you need.

This approach is what I call "failing forward." It shifts the goal from getting it "right" the first time to learning quickly and adapting intelligently. It requires humility, patience, and a willingness to think differently about how we work with technology. Yes, this new way of thinking can feel intimidating. We're conditioned to imagine AI in terms of dystopian fiction, more Terminator than teammate. But the future of AI isn't about domination. It's about collaboration.

I like to think of these tools as more Wall-E than Terminator. Friendly, helpful, task-focused systems that are here to serve, not replace. In fact, the tool manufacturer DeWalt has two robots in its production line, and the employees affectionately refer to them as *"co-bots"* rather than robots. Why? Because robots replace you. Co-bots work with you. They take on repetitive, time-consuming tasks so that people can focus on what humans do best—solving problems, building relationships, and creating strategy.[85]

That's the kind of relationship we need to build with our data systems and AI tools. They're not here to take over—they are here to unlock capacity. But that only works if we're willing to try, fail, learn, and try again. If you're leading in this space, you don't have to be the expert. But you do have to be the one willing to stay in the process, to model resilience, and to help your team develop confidence using these tools. The future of work requires iteration, not perfection. And that's a skill every leader can cultivate.

TAKE ACTION

The future of data-driven marketing in higher ed belongs to leaders who ask better questions, embrace new technologies, and collaborate intentionally to solve meaningful problems. The following exercises and reflection points are designed to help you apply the ideas from this chapter to your unique context. Take time to work through them, either on your own or with your team, and use them as a springboard for meaningful conversations and actionable insights.

Reflective Questions

- Where in your institution are data silos holding you back from seeing the full picture?
- What are the recurring questions your team struggles to answer because of access, time, or tools?
- When was the last time you asked a question that led to real, actionable insight?
- How do you model curiosity and critical thinking for your team?
- What would change if you treated your data tools like collaborators rather than just systems?

Action Steps

- Identify how many databases your institution is using and which teams can access which data. Start mapping out where silos exist.

- Test a Co-Bot tool by selecting one AI tool (for data analysis, outreach, or student support) and test it on a single process or report. Focus on iteration and learning, not perfection.
- Host a prompting workshop to help your team improve how they frame questions and prompts for AI or data tools. Start with one initiative, like enrollment marketing, and explore how better questions lead to better results.
- The next time a tool or report doesn't deliver what you hoped, walk your team through the "fail forward" approach. Reframe the question, adjust the inputs, and try again.

13

COURAGEOUS LEADERSHIP

"Leadership and learning are indispensable to each other."
— John F. Kennedy

THERE WAS A TIME when running a small, private college felt like fishing in a well-stocked pond. You didn't have to chase leads or campaign for attention. You simply cast your line, waited, and reeled in the students who were already there.

The model was simple. Serve the local community, draw from your denominational ties, and trust that enough students would show up to keep things running. Through the '80s and '90s, that worked. The job of admissions wasn't to drum up demand, it was to sort the mail, answer the phone, and respond to interest that already existed. Leadership, back then, was about guarding the mission. You were a steward, not a seller. If students came, they came. If they didn't, well—maybe next year. But those days are gone.

Sometime between the rise of the internet and the fall of Blockbuster, everything changed. Students no longer waited for institutions to find them. They started searching for the best-fit experience, wherever it might be. When I was a student, the way we discovered an institution was through a little magazine called *Campus Life*. Every issue came with a calling card in the back where you could check boxes for the colleges you were interested in and send it off in the mail. Those colleges would get notified that you were interested, and they would reach out. It was low-tech, slow-motion marketing, but it worked because the institutions were in control.

Today? That message is a Google search away. A prospective student can type "best colleges for digital media" or "best nursing programs" and instantly uncover hundreds of institutions they've never heard of. The discovery process has flipped. Students are in the driver's seat now, and that means higher education leaders can't wait for interest. They have to start actively generating it.

This is the moment when mission meets market, and it's a shift that requires institutional leaders to change the way they think. Many presidents are still deep in the academic trenches, fluent in faculty governance, but hesitant to touch words like "sales," "marketing," or "revenue." I've had presidents confide in me, saying, "I don't know anything about marketing." And I understand the hesitation, but that doesn't mean they can afford to bury their head in the sand.

If you earned a PhD in 17th-century French literature or in constitutional law or in organic chemistry or really anything else that requires a PhD, you are more than capable of learning how to ask the right questions about enrollment, branding, and retention. You're already an expert in something complicated. You know how to think critically, synthesize ideas, and make hard decisions. That means you have what it takes to lead courageously in a context where those skills are desperately needed.

It's this courageous leadership that will help you hit your numbers. Because if you don't, it doesn't just affect this year. It affects the next four. A weak freshman class in 2025 means budget gaps until 2029. Have two or three bad years in a row, and suddenly, you're not steering the ship anymore, you're bailing water, hoping it doesn't sink.

Courageous leadership means acknowledging that the rules have changed and choosing to learn the game rather than sit on the sidelines. No one expects you to be a CMO. But institutional leaders can no longer afford to be passive observers. The future of your institution depends on your willingness to embrace the full weight of your role, as a CEO, steward, strategist—and yes, sometimes, salesperson.

ENERGY OVER EGO

Most people don't pursue leadership roles because they dream of managing budgets or building org charts. They arrive in these roles because they were exceptional at something. It could be teaching, research, strategy, or relationships, and at some point, someone recognized that strength and said, "You should be in charge."

But just because you've stepped into a leadership role doesn't mean you have to be great at everything. In fact, trying to be all things to all people is one of the fastest ways to burn out and to slow everyone else down. Leadership isn't about being the expert in every room. It's about knowing your lane, owning it, and building a team that complements it.

That starts with getting real about what you're actually good at. For me, I figured out pretty quickly that I'm at my best when I'm in the room with people, talking through problems and helping them see the bigger picture. That's my lane. That's why I called my company *Caylor Solutions*—because that's what I do. I listen, I understand, I help solve. But not everything I do is in that lane. I can write. I can design. I've even done some solid web development in my day. But that's not where I shine, and it's definitely not what gives me energy.

When you're running an institution (or any business) you've got to pay attention to what energizes you. In Jim Loehr's book, *The Power of Full Engagement*,[86] he talks about energy management. He said, "Energy, not time, is the fundamental currency of high performance." And that, "To be fully engaged, we must be physically energized, emotionally connected, mentally focused and spiritually aligned with a purpose beyond our immediate self-interest."

You can do something for eight hours and be totally depleted, or you can do something else for the same amount of time and walk away buzzing. That matters. So, I started hiring people who were better than me at the things that drained me.

When I hired Beth Mills, I was looking for a bookkeeper to help me stay organized. What I didn't expect was that she would become so much more than that. Beth's project management skills and strategic thinking not only made her my go-to for decisions I didn't want to make alone, but she also laid the foundation for the way Caylor Solutions operates today. In many ways, the growth of our company is built on the systems and stability she helped create.

Later, I brought in Hanna Wilson as my Vice President and Chief of Staff. She runs the team, oversees the management of our projects, and keeps the train running on time so I can focus on what only I can do. Even for this very book in your hands, I hired someone to help me create it. I'm a decent writer, sure. But writing a whole book? That takes a different kind of discipline, and I knew that wasn't my strength. So, I brought in a ghostwriter, Danielle Harward, to help me do it right.

It's the same principle Jim Collins talks about in his book *Good to Great*.[87] He says, "The executives who ignited the transformations from good to great did not first figure out where to drive the bus and then get people to take it there. No, they first got the right people on the bus (and the wrong people off the bus) and then figured out where to drive it." As the leader, you're driving the bus. That means it's your job to know who's good at what, and that includes yourself.

I'm not saying this is easy. It takes humility to admit you're not the best person for every job. But that's the whole point. You don't have to be. You just have to know where you're strong and where you need backup.

I like *Gallup StrengthsFinder*[88] for that reason. It gives you language for your instincts. My top five are strategic, ideation, futuristic, empathy, and activator, but I'm not strong in the details, and my team knows it. So, they don't ask me to proofread things, but they do ask me to help them connect the dots, push a strategy forward, or spot the real issue buried under the surface. That's the stuff I do well. That's where I'm most useful. So, I've shifted my workload to help me focus more on that work.

If you want to lead well, start by getting clear on what you're not good at, and what depletes your energy. Then build a team that fills in the gaps.

THE BUSINESS OF BEING HONEST

If you lead in higher ed today, you've probably heard the term "courageous leadership" before. Johanna Soliday from Credo wrote a whole book about it titled *Surviving to Thriving: A Planning Framework for Leaders of Private Colleges and Universities*.[89] And she's right to frame it that way. These days, surviving does take courage, and thriving takes even more. In her book she said, "The most important element to the health of an institution in today's urgent times is a strong and capable leadership team." She went on to add that, "College presidents must be courageous enough to embrace the means to true student success if we really wish to have distinctive and authentic value propositions. This issue is not just about increasing a retention percentage or improving customer service. Student learning and success is at the center of everything we believe in. When approached with intentionality and consistency, it will transform our students, and through them, the world."

Most of us leaders didn't sign up to be the bad guy. We like collaboration. We like shared governance. We're part of an ecosystem that, at its best, is meant to be egalitarian—where every voice matters and every program has value. But running a college isn't just an academic exercise anymore. It's a business. And in any business, not all products have equal demand.

That's where courageous leadership shows up. It's not just about making decisions. It's about making the ones you know will upset people and doing it anyway because it's the right call for the future of the institution. It means acknowledging what the market is asking for and not being afraid to pivot toward it. It means saying hard things out loud, letting people be upset, and standing by your decisions anyway. It's not easy. It's not always popular. But it's necessary.

When you lead with courage, you're going to make some people uncomfortable. You might even make some enemies. But you can't let that stop you. Because if your priority is popularity, you're not leading, you're managing feelings. And that's not going to save your institution.

At the end of the day, courageous leadership is about stewardship. Stewardship of your mission. Stewardship of your people. And stewardship of your resources. That means making tough calls that protect the whole, even if it stings in the short term.

THE COST OF KICKING THE CAN

When I sit down with presidents or VPs and ask, "What's more important, getting through this year or securing the long-term health of your institution?", most people answer the way you'd expect. Of course, they say, the future matters more.

But then we start talking about strategy, suddenly it's all about closing this year's class, patching this year's budget, and surviving this season.

It's not that higher education leaders don't care about the long-term. It's that the pressure of the short-term is *relentless*. In higher ed, where cycles repeat every year like clockwork, it's incredibly easy to kick the can down the road. Just make it through this class. Just hold on one more year. Just renew that one contract. Just keep the ad campaign running. Until one day, you can't.

I've seen it happen more times than I'd like. Institutions that avoided hard choices for so long that eventually, the only choice left was to close the campus. And when that happens, it's rarely because of one big decision. It's a hundred small ones—unmade, unchecked, and left to snowball.

There's one institution I worked with that during my assessment audit, we discovered they had a digital ad campaign running in their Google account for *seventeen years*. Seventeen. It was spending $1,000 a month, and nobody was actively managing it. It just kept renewing, year after year, because no one took the time to pause, evaluate, and ask, "Is this still working?" That's over $200,000 spent because it was easier to leave it than to deal with it.[90]

Now, someone might argue that was a decision, they decided to keep going. But I'd push back on that. Did you really decide to keep it going? Or did you avoid deciding because you didn't understand the tool well enough to ask the right questions?

Avoiding a decision isn't neutral. It has a cost. Courageous leadership means making the small, hard decisions now so you don't find yourself boxed into an impossible one later. It means pulling the plug on what isn't working, even if it's easier to let it ride. It means saying, "Let's fix this," instead of, "Let's survive this." The decisions you delay today will compound, and eventually, they'll make the decision for you.

CURIOSITY IS A LEADERSHIP SKILL

If any industry should champion curiosity, it's higher education. After all, *this is an industry built on questions.* The earliest universities weren't founded to crank out credentials. They were born out of a hunger to understand the world through science, theology, debate, and dialogue. They were communities of inquiry. People came together to ask big, sometimes uncomfortable questions about how things work and why we're here.

But somewhere along the way, the business side of the house became more about having answers than asking questions. In a space where certainty is often equated with competence, it's easy to feel like you need to have everything figured out before walking into the room. Over time, curiosity gave way to caution because the stakes felt too high to admit what they didn't know.

I've sat with leaders who didn't want to ask a single question about marketing because they were afraid it would make them look uninformed. Others have disengaged entirely—hands off, eyes down—because somewhere along the way, they decided their learning had a finish line. And look, I get it. When your plate's full and the board's breathing down your neck, it's tempting to nod along and hope nobody notices you don't know what a CRM actually does. But the truth is, *you're not supposed to know everything*. You're supposed to keep learning. Your job isn't to become an expert in SEO, or ad buying, or conversion funnels. Your job is to get curious enough to ask the right questions, so the experts on your team can do their best work.

Curiosity isn't a luxury; it's a leadership requirement. Especially now. I hope, if nothing else, this book gives you permission to lean into that. To raise your hand. To say, "Help me understand this better."

When you stay curious, you lead differently. You engage more. You make better decisions. And you give your team permission to be honest with you because they know you're there to learn. If higher ed leadership forgets how to be curious, we lose the very thing that made it worth protecting in the first place.

As this book comes to a close, I ask you to make courageous leadership a priority. When you feel yourself pulling back, lean in. If you wonder if asking a question will make you look uninformed, make it a priority to ask so you can start seeing those moments as opportunities. Now is the time to make that curiosity work for you, and for your institution. Because you never know what you don't know.

TAKE ACTION

Courageous leadership isn't flashy. But it is vital. It helps you see the full picture so you can lead your institution through any storm. The following exercises and reflection points are designed to help you apply the ideas from this chapter to your unique context. Take time to work through them, either on your own or with your team, and use them as a springboard for meaningful conversations and actionable insights.

Reflective Questions

- Where am I kicking the can down the road instead of facing a hard decision head-on?
- What part of my role energizes me most? Where do I feel drained—and why?
- What conversations am I avoiding because I fear they'll be unpopular?
- Where have I stopped being curious? What am I pretending to understand, instead of asking more questions?

Action Steps

- Take a week to jot down what tasks or meetings energize you and which ones leave you depleted. Look for patterns and opportunities to delegate what drains you.
- Audit one area you've been avoiding. Maybe it's your digital marketing spend. Maybe it's program prioriti-

zation. Pick one place where you've been deferring and make a decision this month.

- Ask one "dumb" question and do it publicly. Model curiosity. Give your team permission to be learners again by leading the way.
- Talk to your team about courageous leadership. Bring this chapter to a leadership meeting. Use it to open a conversation about the decisions you *aren't* making and what's holding you back.
- Ask yourself who on your team is in the wrong seat? Who's got more to give but hasn't been asked? Start shifting based on strengths, not just job titles, so you can get the right people in the right seat.

CONCLUSION: PHRONESIS

THERE'S A GREEK WORD I love, *phronesis.* It refers to practical wisdom or intelligence, associated with the ability to discern what is appropriate in a given situation. It's the difference between knowing the textbook definition of "lead generation" and actually knowing how to get prospective students to fill out your inquiry form.

Now, I'm not a Greek scholar by any stretch, but I do love words like this one. Words that give shape to something we've all felt. Because right now we're living in a time when leaders are expected to know more than ever before—and faster than ever before, too. You're supposed to be familiar with marketing funnels, enrollment trends, tech stacks, AI, UX, ROI, brand voice, and maybe still find time to attend a student pancake breakfast. No one handed you a playbook. No one trained you for this moment. That can feel overwhelming. And worse, it can feel like you're not allowed to admit what you don't know.

But you don't know what you don't know. And that isn't a bad thing. In fact, it's the opposite. Good leaders don't pretend to have all the answers. They build the muscle of asking the right questions. They know how to find people they can trust. They stay curious, especially when the stakes are high. That spirit of inquiry, of intellectual humility, is baked into the DNA of higher education. The academy has always been a place for exploration. We encourage our students to ask bold questions, to challenge assumptions, to learn deeply, and to think critically. So, why do we so often deny ourselves that same grace?

You don't need a doctorate in marketing to be an effective higher ed leader. You don't need to be a digital advertising expert or a web analytics wizard. What you do need is the willingness to dig in, to understand just enough to make informed decisions, and to build relationships with people who've walked the road before you. In many ways, it's no different from the structure of a dissertation. You don't invent everything from scratch. You stand on the shoulders of others. You do the reading, the research, the interviews. You take meaning from what you gather and then you apply it to your specific context.

Now, you don't have to go read all the literature out there. I've designed this book to be enough for you to get your bearings. It will act as a frame for understanding the marketing fundamentals you need to move the needle. But more than that, I hope it's offered you some encouragement. Because this work is hard. It's easy to feel isolated or behind. But you're not alone. There's a whole *ecosystem* of trusted guides, thoughtful partners, and fellow learners out there. People who aren't just looking to sell you a product, but who are ready to walk alongside you as you navigate this complex space.

That's the kind of work I've tried to do throughout my career. I'm not interested in being just another vendor. I don't want to sell you a product and disappear. I want to roll up my sleeves, understand your mission, and walk alongside you to get the results that matter most. This is often the difference between starting a new hobby on your own and muddling your way through versus having someone who is experienced show you how to do it successfully from the start. For example, if you want to learn to flyfish, you can go to Walmart and buy fishing gear, then make your way to a body of water and give it a try. Or you can hire a guide who knows the river, knows where the fish bite, and knows the obstacles you'll need to navigate.

Whether it's me or someone else, *find your guide*. Marketing in higher ed isn't like marketing anywhere else. You're not selling gym memberships. You're not hawking widgets. You're not putting up a billboard for the carwash that everyone will eventually need. You're trying to connect students to life paths, and not every student is the right fit for your institution. That's why you have to market differently.

If you're a college president who needs a sounding board, call me. If you know more about enrollment than marketing, I can help bridge that gap. If you're new to higher ed leadership and still figuring out the landscape, let's talk. The first call is always free, no strings attached. Sometimes that turns into a consulting retainer. Sometimes it turns into a project with my team. But sometimes, you just need to vent and get some clarity, and I'm happy to be that person for you.

Whatever your next step looks like, know this: You don't have to be the expert, but you do have to keep learning. I believe you have what it takes to do this work. I believe you can do it well. Every strong leader I know started by admitting what they didn't know and then began doing the work to learn it. If you can do that, there's no limit to the impact you can make.

ACKNOWLEDGMENTS

WRITING A BOOK IS NEVER A SOLO EFFORT. This one, in particular, has been shaped and supported by so many people whose fingerprints are all over these pages.

To Kelly Hiller and Emily Richwine of Purdue University, I am grateful for your permission to tell your stories so others can learn from your leadership. I'm also thankful to Matt Osborne and Peter Samuelson of Ardeo for introducing me to Jeremy Taylor, whose story of Defiance College's turnaround is one I'll never forget. And to Erik Ankerberg, I deeply appreciate your humility and trust in letting me bring our conversation into these pages.

A big thank you to Ashley Monk and Silvia Lucaschi-Decker, who graciously checked the numbers in Chapter Six and ensured the data was both accurate and practical. I appreciate your critical eye and willingness to take the time.

Closer to home, I'm grateful for my leadership team—Hannah Wilson, Zach Coffin, and Becca Coffin—who keep pushing Caylor Solutions forward with insights, input, and hard work. And to the many guests of the Higher Ed Marketer Podcast, thank you for challenging me, teaching me, and sharpening the way I think about higher education marketing.

To my cheerleaders who show up online, in person, and in spirit, your encouragement has kept me going. Tyler Groepper, Chris Rapozo, Luke Phillips, Troy Singer, the "Crossroads Crew" (Brad Ward, Jeremy Tiers, Ryan Barbauld, Soup Campbell), Brad Entwistle of ImageSeven, Dave Burke, David Medders, Carol Dibble, Philip Dearborn, and countless others who have encouraged me, I'm grateful for each of you.

A special shout-out goes to Jaime and Dave Hunt, my faithful "texting buddies." You're always there when the "I can't believe this just happened" moments roll in, and your friendship has reminded me time and again why good questions matter.

To Danielle Harward, thank you for shepherding me through another book and helping me shape my words into something cohesive and useful. To all the reviewers who lent their expertise and endorsement, I am truly grateful.

Finally, to my family, your love and support make everything possible. And most of all, I am grateful to the Father, Son, and Holy Spirit, from whom all blessings flow. *Colossians 3:23*

NOTES

INTRODUCTION

1 *Apollo 13.* (2025, September 17). Retrieved from Wikipedia: https://en.wikipedia.org/wiki/Apollo_13

CHAPTER 1

2 *Trust, but verify.* (2025, 11 September). Retrieved from Wikipedia: https://en.wikipedia.org/wiki/Trust,_but_verify#:~:text=distrust%20 and%20verify%22.-,Origins,a%20good%20basis%20for%20 cooperation%22%20.

3 Perrin, C. P. (2014, 11 March). *Good Colleges for Classically-Educated Students.* Retrieved from Inside Classical Education: https:// insideclassicaled.com/good-colleges-for-classically-educated-students/

4 *Radio Shack.* (2025, 15 September). Retrieved from Wikipedia: https://en.wikipedia.org/wiki/RadioShack

5 *DOS.* (2025, 11 September). Retrieved from Wikipedia: https:// en.wikipedia.org/wiki/DOS

6 *Steve Jobs.* (2025, 26 September). Retrieved from Wikipedia: https://en.wikipedia.org/wiki/Steve_Jobs

7 *Steve Wozniak.* (2025, 26 September). Retrieved from Wikipedia: https://en.wikipedia.org/wiki/Steve_Wozniak

8   *Macintosh 128K.* (2025, 24 September). Retrieved from Wikipedia: https://en.wikipedia.org/wiki/Macintosh_128K

9   *ZeeMee.* (2025). Retrieved from ZeeMee: https://www.zeemee.com/

CHAPTER 2

10   Wells, P. C. (2024). *Clever Marketing Explained: Circus Analogy for Small Business Owners.* Retrieved from YouTube: https://www.youtube.com/watch?v=pxKIv6d2Xo4

11   *Drucker, Peter F.* . (2024). Retrieved from Marketing Insider Group: marketinginsidergroup.com

12   Hint: If you've read my previous book, Chasing Mission Fit, you've heard this analogy before. I can't help but use it again here because it's so relevant.

13   Some institutions are exploring tuition resets, where they slash the sticker price dramatically in hopes of appearing more affordable. From a marketing perspective, I'm not a fan. While it might generate short-term buzz, it often creates long-term confusion and can actually add friction. Students and families are left wondering if the value has changed, or why it was so high to begin with. I'm not opposed to tuition discounting, but we need to present it in a way that clearly communicates what students will actually pay. Clarity beats drama every time.

14   Lederman, D. (2019, June 4). *Online Is (Increasingly) Local.* Retrieved from Inside Higher Ed: https://www.insidehighered.com/digital-learning/article/2019/06/05/annual-survey-shows-online-college-students-increasingly

15   If you're thinking, "I don't have enough time to handle all that research!" I encourage you to read my previous book, Chasing Mission Fit, where I discuss what should (and shouldn't) be in the marketing department's purview. I also offer some tips for how to offload work the marketing department shouldn't be doing.

16   Fletcher, A. (2023). *Storythinking: The New Science of Narrative Intelligence (No Limits).* Columbia University Press.

17   Hall, K. (2019). *Stories That Stick: How Storytelling Can Captivate Customers, Influence Audiences, and Transform Your Business.* HarperCollins Leadership.

CHAPTER 3

18   Gregoire, E. (2024, October 24). *AI Adoption in 2024: 74% of Companies Struggle to Achieve and Scale Value.* Retrieved from Boston Consulting Group: https://www.bcg.com/press/24october2024-ai-adoption-in-2024-74-of-companies-struggle-to-achieve-and-scale-value#:~:text=Leaders%20Far%20Outperform%20the%20Rest%20Over%20the,areas%20like%20patents%20filed%20and%20employee%20satisfaction\

19   Caylor, B. (2025). *AI in Marketing.* Routledge.

20   Abando, I. Z. (2024, December 19). *Why AI Is More Than Just "The New Electricity".* Retrieved from LinkedIn: https://www.linkedin.com/pulse/why-ai-more-than-just-new-electricity-iker-zubizarreta-abando-dntzc/

21   Haroon Sheikh, C. P. (2023, January 31). *AI as a System Technology.* Retrieved from https://link.springer.com/chapter/10.1007/978-3-031-21448-6_4

22   *Artificial Intelligence.* (2025). Retrieved from Arizona State University: https://ai.asu.edu/

23   Heller, S. (2020, November 23). *The Daily Heller: Stephen Alcorn's Great Masters Lesson.* Retrieved from Print Mag: https://www.printmag.com/daily-heller/the-daily-heller-stephen-alcorn-s-great-masters-lesson/

24   Woodie, M. (2017). *10 Master Drawers (and What They Teach Us).* Retrieved from Artists Network: https://www.artistsnetwork.com/art-history/masters-10-great-drawers-and-what-they-teach-us/

25   *Arthur C. Clarke.* (2025, May 18). Retrieved from Wikipedia: https://en.wikiquote.org/wiki/Arthur_C._Clarke

26   Godin, S. (2025). Retrieved from Canva: https://www.canva.com/design/DAGmgEss5dY/v1n71ng0_WbF-BYnocWsLw/view?utm_content=DAGmgEss5dY&utm_campaign=designshare&utm_medium=link2&utm_source=uniquelinks&utlId=h9520130c2a

27   Caylor, B. (2025). Retrieved from LinkedIn: https://www.linkedin.com/posts/bartcaylor_gemini-chatgpt-activity-7274466182043250689-KRS3/?utm_source=share&utm_medium=member_desktop

CHAPTER 4

28   I recently wrote a LinkedIn post on this topic. In it, I discuss the thumbs up emoji. Gen Z considers this the rudest emoji as it feels passive-aggressive and sarcastic. They also see it as "officially old" when used, and 25% of those surveyed found it the "uncoolest" emoji of them all.

29   Gladwell, M. (2024). *Revenge of the Tipping Point: Overstories, Superspreaders, and the Rise of Social Engineering.* Little, Brown & Company.

30   (ClipCafe, 1985) (1985). Retrieved from ClipCafe: https://clip.cafe/back-the-future-1985/then-tell-future-boy-s1/

31   Megan Gerhardt, J. N.-E. (2021). *Gentelligence: The Revolutionary Approach to Leading an Intergenerational Workforce.* Rowman & Littlefield Publishers.

32   (2023). Retrieved from TikTok: https://www.tiktok.com/@caitconquers/video/7235784818372529450

33   Vaynerchuk, G. (2024). *Day Trading Attention: How to Actually Build Brand and Sales in the New Social Media World.* Harper Business.

34   RCA was once a household name in consumer electronics, familiar to Gen X and Boomers as a major TV and stereo brand. But for Millennials and Gen Z, the name often doesn't register at all. That gap in recognition is itself a reminder of how quickly brands can fade from cultural memory, and why generational context matters in marketing.

35   Little, B. (2018). *When Cigarette Companies Used Doctors to Push Smoking.* Retrieved from History: https://www.history.com/articles/cigarette-ads-doctors-smoking-endorsement

36   *Collection: More Doctors Smoke Camels.* (2025). Retrieved from Stanford: https://tobacco.stanford.edu/cigarettes/doctors-smoking/more-doctors-smoke-camels/

37   In my previous book, Chasing Mission Fit, I delver deeper into watering holes and how higher education marketing leaders can use them to their advantage. Check it out if you would like to dive deeper on this topic.

38   I know I've referenced my previous book, Chasing Mission Fit, a few times already, but if you need more detail on how to shift away from this type of selling into a more target focus on your mission-fit student it really is the book for you.

CHAPTER 5

39   Sinek, S. (2025). *Start with Why (15th Anniversary Edition): How Great Leaders Inspire Everyone to Take Action.* Penguin. Retrieved from https://simonsinek.com/books/start-with-why/

40   If you need help defining who your audience is, check out chapter one of my previous book, *Chasing Mission Fit*. In that chapter I define exactly how to find your mission-fit student and refine your watering holes.

41   *Inside the Enrollment Playbook: Data, Strategy, and Bold Moves.* (2025, February 25). Retrieved from The Higher Ed Marketer: https://thehigheredmarketer.com/episodes/inside-the-enrollment-playbook-data-strategy-and-bold-moves/

42   Carnegie, D. (1998). *How to Win Friends & Influence People.* Pocket Books.

43   *Field of Dreams.* (n.d.). Retrieved from IMDB: https://www.imdb.com/title/tt0097351/

44   My favorite tools are ChatGPT and Perplexity. Of course, that could change tomorrow with how rapidly new AI technologies are coming about.

CHAPTER 6

45   *2019 Recruitment and Yield Rate Benchmarks for Four-Year Institutions.* (2019). Retrieved from RNL: https://learn.ruffalonl.com/rs/395-EOG-977/images/2019_Conversion%20and%20Yield%20Report_EM-008.pdf

46   *Pay Per Click.* (2025, August 11). Retrieved from Wikipedia: https://en.wikipedia.org/wiki/Pay-per-click

47   Long-tail keywords are search terms with lower competition but higher intent. Things like your school's name, unique program offerings, or specific questions that prospective students might ask.

48   *Higher Education PPC.* (2021). Retrieved from Reddit: https://www.reddit.com/r/PPC/comments/qndsee/higher_education_ppc/?rdt=39310

49   Relic, J. (2025, September 25). *How Much Does Google Ads Cost in 2025? Full Pricing Guide.* Retrieved from Ninja Promo: https://ninjapromo.io/how-much-does-google-ads-cost

50   French, P. (2024, November 26). *Understanding Cost Per Inquiry in Higher Education Marketing.* Retrieved from The Online and Professional Education Association: https://upcea.edu/understanding-cost-per-inquiry-in-higher-education-marketing/

51   Khan, F. (2024). *Navigating Google Ads in 2024: A Guide for Higher Education Marketers.* Retrieved from LinkedIn: https://www.linkedin.com/pulse/navigating-google-ads-2024-guide-higher-education-marketers-khan-iingc/

52   Emma, L. (2020). *Why Google Keywords Are So Expensive for Higher Education.* Retrieved from Cloud Control Media: https://cloudcontrolmedia.com/blog/why-google-keyword-expensive-higher-education/

53   Wood, M. (2024). *Why Long-Tail Keywords Will Dominate SEO Strategies in 2025.* Retrieved from The Hoth: https://www.thehoth.com/blog/long-tail-keyword-seo/

CHAPTER 7

54   *2025 E-Expectations® Trend Report.* (2025). Retrieved from RNL: https://www.ruffalonl.com/papers-research-higher-education-fundraising/e-expectations/

55   If you'd like more in depth information on how to answer these questions through your copy, check out chapter six of my previous book, *Chasing Mission Fit.*

56   God created these so we could explain things in small print.

57   *About Ivy Tech.* (2025). Retrieved from Ivy Tech Community College: https://www.ivytech.edu/about-ivy-tech/

58   *Strategic Plan.* (2025). Retrieved from Ivy Tech Community College: https://www.ivytech.edu/about-ivy-tech/college-operations/strategic-plan/

59   Miller, D. (2017). *Building a StoryBrand: Clarify Your Message So Customers Will Listen.* HarperCollins Leadership.

60   Pelia, H. S. (2024). *The Psychology of Marketing: How Marketers Trick Us Into Buying More.* Notion Press.

61   If you want to email me at Caylor solutions to ask questions on what you are currently working through, I'll jump on a 15 minute call for free to talk about it because it pains me to see schools making bad decisions when they don't what they don't know.

CHAPTER 8

62   Lencioni, P. M. (2012). *The Advantage: Why Organizational Health Trumps Everything Else In Business.* Jossey-Bass.

63   Tymoshchuk, O. (2021). *Font Readability Research: Key Difference Between Serif Vs Sans Serif Font.* Retrieved from Geniusee: https://geniusee.com/single-blog/font-readability-research-famous-designers-vs-scientists

64   Check out our The Higher Ed Marketer Podcast where we discuss tapping into student expertise with Mary here: https://thehigheredmarketer.com/episodes/transition-reaction-tapping-student-expertise-w-mary-barr/.

65   Carnegie, D. (1998). *How to Win Friends & Influence People.* Pocket Books.

66   Godin, S. (2012). *All Marketers are Liars: The Underground Classic That Explains How Marketing Really Works--and Why Authenticity Is the Best Marketing of All.* Portfolio.

CHAPTER 9

67   Caylor, B. (2025). *Enhancing Institutional Marketing Strategies for Success.* Retrieved from Loom: https://www.loom.com/share/628a3bc2c13b4694b97c93be69a51e3b

68　*Purdue Brand Studio Earns Global Recognition.* (2025). Retrieved from Purdue University: https://marcom.purdue.edu/impact/recognition/

69　Renton, K. (2024). *QuickFire: Jenny Petty.* Retrieved from Volt: https://voltedu.com/virtual-interviews/quickfire-jenny-petty/

70　Ultimately, the student is fully committed until the minivan drives away and census is taken in the early weeks of September. I would also argue that marketing needs to work with Student life on retention strategies for that crucial first semester and return after the holidays.

71　*Research on the Prospective College Student Campus Visit and Its Impact on Matriculation.* (2025). Retrieved from BHDP: https://www.bhdp.com/insights/research-prospective-college-student-campus-visit-and-its-impact-matriculation

72　Donadel, A. (2023). *Here are 2 ways to curb high admission officer turnover rates.* Retrieved from University Business: https://universitybusiness.com/here-are-2-ways-to-curb-high-admission-officer-turnover-rates/

CHAPTER 10

73　*Branding Our Next Giant Leap.* (2022). Retrieved from Purdue University: https://marcom.purdue.edu/app/uploads/2022/02/brand-strategy-guideline.pdf

74　A great resource that makes the point: https://www.insidehighered.com/news/2016/05/02/why-colleges%E2%80%99-brands-look-so-similar

CHAPTER 11

75　Andrivet, M. (2025). *New Coke: A Classic Branding Case Study on a Major Product Change Failure.* Retrieved from The Branding Journal: https://www.thebrandingjournal.com/2025/02/new-coke/

76　Caylor, B. (2024). *A Business-Like Approach: Bringing a CEO Mindset to Higher Ed.* Retrieved from The Higher Ed Marketer: https://thehigheredmarketer.com/episodes/a-business-like-approach-bringing-a-ceo-mindset-to-higher-ed/

77   Caylor, B. (2022). *The Key to Successful Content Marketing*. Retrieved from The Higher Ed Marketer: https://thehigheredmarketer.com/episodes/the-key-to-successful-content-marketing/

78   Baer, J. (2023). *The Time to Win: How to Exceed Your Customers' Need for Speed*. Ursus 10 Media.

79   Welding, L. (2025). *College Graduation Rates: Full Statistics*. Retrieved from Best Colleges: https://www.bestcolleges.com/research/college-graduation-rates/

80   Guidara, W. (2022). *Unreasonable Hospitality: The Remarkable Power of Giving People More Than They Expect*. Optimism Press.

81   Joe Messinger, C. (2023). *Why Are Students Dropping Out of College?* Retrieved from Capstone Wealth Partners: https://capstonewealthpartners.com/why-are-students-dropping-out-of-college/

82   Caylor, B. (2024). *Life Skills, AI, and Innovation with Dr. Nido Qubein from High Point University*. Retrieved from The Higher Ed Marketer: https://thehigheredmarketer.com/episodes/life-skills-ai-and-innovation-with-dr-nido-qubein-from-high-point-university/

83   (2023). Retrieved from Instagram: https://www.instagram.com/reel/C0xPf94uwVL/?igshid=MzRlODBiNWFlZA%3D%3D

CHAPTER 12

84   Duhigg, C. (2014). *The Power of Habit: Why We Do What We Do in Life and Business* . Random House Trade Paperbacks.

85   (n.d.). Retrieved from PRNEWSWIRE: https://www.prnewswire.com/news-releases/an-inside-look-into-manufacturing-dewalt-power-tools-stanley-black--decker-is-featured-in-upcoming-modern-marvels-machines-episode-airing-on-the-history-channel-301351086.html

CHAPTER 13

86   Loehr, J. (2003). *The Power of Full Engagement: Managing Energy, Not Time, Is the Key to High Performance and Personal Renewal*. Free Press.

87   Collins, J. (2001). *Good to Great: Why Some Companies Make the Leap...And Others Don't.* Harper Business.

88   Gallup. (2007). *StrengthsFinder 2.0.* Gallup Press.

89   Soliday, J., & Mann, R. (2018). *Surviving To Thriving: A Planning Framework for Leaders of Private Colleges & Universities.* Advantage Media Group.

90   No, this isn't the same institution that spent $1,200 on a keyword! There are plenty of institutions making this mistake and money slipping through the gaps. If you'd like an audit for your school, I can help.

BIBLIOGRAPHY

(n.d.). Retrieved from PRNEWSWIRE: https://www.prnewswire.com/news-releases/an-inside-look-into-manufacturing-dewalt-power-tools-stanley-black--decker-is-featured-in-upcoming-modern-marvels-machines-episode-airing-on-the-history-channel-301351086.html

(1985). Retrieved from ClipCafe: https://clip.cafe/back-the-future-1985/then-tell-future-boy-s1/

2019 Recruitment and Yield Rate Benchmarks for Four-Year Institutions. (2019). Retrieved from RNL: https://learn.ruffalonl.com/rs/395-EOG-977/images/2019_Conversion%20and%20Yield%20Report_EM-008.pdf

(2023). Retrieved from TikTok: https://www.tiktok.com/@caitconquers/video/7235784818372529450

(2023). Retrieved from Instagram: https://www.instagram.com/reel/C0xPf94uwVL/?igshid=MzRlODBiNWFlZA%3D%3D

2025 E-Expectations® Trend Report. (2025). Retrieved from RNL: https://www.ruffalonl.com/papers-research-higher-education-fundraising/e-expectations/

Abando, I. Z. (2024, December 19). *Why AI Is More Than Just "The New Electricity".* Retrieved from LinkedIn: https://www.linkedin.com/pulse/why-ai-more-than-just-new-electricity-iker-zubizarreta-abando-dntzc/

About Ivy Tech. (2025). Retrieved from Ivy Tech Community College: https://www.ivytech.edu/about-ivy-tech/

Andrivet, M. (2025). *New Coke: A Classic Branding Case Study on a Major Product Change Failure*. Retrieved from The Branding Journal: https://www.thebrandingjournal.com/2025/02/new-coke/

Apollo 13. (2025, September 17). Retrieved from Wikipedia: https://en.wikipedia.org/wiki/Apollo_13

Arthur C. Clarke. (2025, May 18). Retrieved from Wikipedia: https://en.wikiquote.org/wiki/Arthur_C._Clarke

Artificial Intelligence. (2025). Retrieved from Arizona State University: https://ai.asu.edu/

Baer, J. (2023). *The Time to Win: How to Exceed Your Customers' Need for Speed*. Ursus 10 Media.

Branding Our Next Giant Leap. (2022). Retrieved from Purdue University: https://marcom.purdue.edu/app/uploads/2022/02/brand-strategy-guideline.pdf

Carnegie, D. (1998). *How to Win Friends & Influence People*. Pocket Books.

Caylor, B. (2022). *The Key to Successful Content Marketing*. Retrieved from The Higher Ed Marketer: https://thehigheredmarketer.com/episodes/the-key-to-successful-content-marketing/

Caylor, B. (2024). *A Business-Like Approach: Bringing a CEO Mindset to Higher Ed*. Retrieved from The Higher Ed Marketer: https://thehigheredmarketer.com/episodes/a-business-like-approach-bringing-a-ceo-mindset-to-higher-ed/

Caylor, B. (2024). *Life Skills, AI, and Innovation with Dr. Nido Qubein from High Point University*. Retrieved from The Higher Ed Marketer: https://thehigheredmarketer.com/episodes/life-skills-ai-and-innovation-with-dr-nido-qubein-from-high-point-university/

Caylor, B. (2025). Retrieved from LinkedIn: https://www.linkedin.com/posts/bartcaylor_gemini-chatgpt-activity-7274466182043250689-KRS3/?utm_source=share&utm_medium=member_desktop

Caylor, B. (2025). *AI in Marketing*. Routledge.

Caylor, B. (2025). *Enhancing Institutional Marketing Strategies for Success*. Retrieved from Loom: https://www.loom.com/share/628a3bc2c13b4694b97c93be69a51e3b

Collection: More Doctors Smoke Camels. (2025). Retrieved from Stanford: https://tobacco.stanford.edu/cigarettes/doctors-smoking/more-doctors-smoke-camels/

Collins, J. (2001). *Good to Great: Why Some Companies Make the Leap... And Others Don't*. Harper Business.

Donadel, A. (2023). *Here are 2 ways to curb high admission officer turnover rates*. Retrieved from University Business: https://universitybusiness.com/here-are-2-ways-to-curb-high-admission-officer-turnover-rates/

DOS. (2025, 11 September). Retrieved from Wikipedia: https://en.wikipedia.org/wiki/DOS

Drucker, Peter F. . (2024). Retrieved from Marketing Insider Group: marketinginsidergroup.com

Duhigg, C. (2014). *The Power of Habit: Why We Do What We Do in Life and Business* . Random House Trade Paperbacks.

Emma, L. (2020). *Why Google Keywords Are So Expensive for Higher Education*. Retrieved from Cloud Control Media: https://cloudcontrolmedia.com/blog/why-google-keyword-expensive-higher-education/

Field of Dreams. (n.d.). Retrieved from IMDB: https://www.imdb.com/title/tt0097351/

Fletcher, A. (2023). *Storythinking: The New Science of Narrative Intelligence (No Limits)*. Columbia University Press.

French, P. (2024, November 26). *Understanding Cost Per Inquiry in Higher Education Marketing*. Retrieved from The Online and Professional Education Association: https://upcea.edu/understanding-cost-per-inquiry-in-higher-education-marketing/

Gallup. (2007). S*trengthsFinder 2.0*. Gallup Press.

Gladwell, M. (2024). *Revenge of the Tipping Point: Overstories, Superspreaders, and the Rise of Social Engineering*. Little, Brown & Company.

Godin, S. (2012). *All Marketers are Liars: The Underground Classic That Explains How Marketing Really Works--and Why Authenticity Is the Best Marketing of All*. Portfolio.

Godin, S. (2025). Retrieved from Canva: https://www.canva.com/design/DAGmgEss5dY/v1n71ng0_WbF-BYnocWsLw/view?utm_content=DAGmgEss5dY&utm_campaign=designshare&utm_medium=link2&utm_source=uniquelinks&utlId=h9520130c2a

Gregoire, E. (2024, October 24). *AI Adoption in 2024: 74% of Companies Struggle to Achieve and Scale Value*. Retrieved from Boston Consulting Group: https://www.bcg.com/press/24october2024-ai-adoption-in-2024-74-of-companies-struggle-to-achieve-and-scale-value#:~:text=Leaders%20Far%20Outperform%20the%20Rest%20Over%20the,areas%20like%20patents%20filed%20and%20employee%20satisfaction

Guidara, W. (2022). *Unreasonable Hospitality: The Remarkable Power of Giving People More Than They Expect*. Optimism Press.

Hall, K. (2019). *Stories That Stick: How Storytelling Can Captivate Customers, Influence Audiences, and Transform Your Business*. HarperCollins Leadership.

Haroon Sheikh, C. P. (2023, January 31). *AI as a System Technology*. Retrieved from https://link.springer.com/chapter/10.1007/978-3-031-21448-6_4

Heller, S. (2020, November 23). *The Daily Heller: Stephen Alcorn's Great Masters Lesson*. Retrieved from Print Mag: https://www.printmag.com/daily-heller/the-daily-heller-stephen-alcorn-s-great-masters-lesson/

Higher Education PPC. (2021). Retrieved from Reddit: https://www.reddit.com/r/PPC/comments/qndsee/higher_education_ppc/?rdt=39310

Inside the Enrollment Playbook: Data, Strategy, and Bold Moves. (2025, February 25). Retrieved from The Higher Ed Marketer: https://thehigheredmarketer.com/episodes/inside-the-enrollment-playbook-data-strategy-and-bold-moves/

Joe Messinger, C. (2023). *Why Are Students Dropping Out of College?* Retrieved from Capstone Wealth Partners: https://capstonewealthpartners.com/why-are-students-dropping-out-of-college/

Khan, F. (2024). *Navigating Google Ads in 2024: A Guide for Higher Education Marketers.* Retrieved from LinkedIn: https://www.linkedin.com/pulse/navigating-google-ads-2024-guide-higher-education-marketers-khan-iingc/

Lederman, D. (2019, June 4). *Online Is (Increasingly) Local.* Retrieved from Inside Higher Ed: https://www.insidehighered.com/digital-learning/article/2019/06/05/annual-survey-shows-online-college-students-increasingly

Lencioni, P. M. (2012). *The Advantage: Why Organizational Health Trumps Everything Else In Business.* Jossey-Bass.

Little, B. (2018). *When Cigarette Companies Used Doctors to Push Smoking.* Retrieved from History: https://www.history.com/articles/cigarette-ads-doctors-smoking-endorsement

Loehr, J. (2003). *The Power of Full Engagement: Managing Energy, Not Time, Is the Key to High Performance and Personal Renewal.* Free Press.

Macintosh 128K. (2025, 24 September). Retrieved from Wikipedia: https://en.wikipedia.org/wiki/Macintosh_128K

Megan Gerhardt, J. N.-E. (2021). *Gentelligence: The Revolutionary Approach to Leading an Intergenerational Workforce.* Rowman & Littlefield Publishers.

Miller, D. (2017). *Building a StoryBrand: Clarify Your Message So Customers Will Listen.* HarperCollins Leadership.

Pay Per Click. (2025, August 11). Retrieved from Wikipedia: https://en.wikipedia.org/wiki/Pay-per-click

Pelia, H. S. (2024). *The Psychology of Marketing: How Marketers Trick Us Into Buying More.* Notion Press.

Perrin, C. P. (2014, 11 March). *Good Colleges for Classically-Educated Students*. Retrieved from Inside Classical Education: https://insideclassicaled.com/good-colleges-for-classically-educated-students/

Purdue Brand Studio Earns Global Recognition. (2025). Retrieved from Purdue University: https://marcom.purdue.edu/impact/recognition/

Radio Shack. (2025, 15 September). Retrieved from Wikipedia: https://en.wikipedia.org/wiki/RadioShack

Relic, J. (2025, September 25). *How Much Does Google Ads Cost in 2025? Full Pricing Guide*. Retrieved from Ninja Promo: https://ninjapromo.io/how-much-does-google-ads-cost

Renton, K. (2024). *QuickFire: Jenny Petty*. Retrieved from Volt: https://voltedu.com/virtual-interviews/quickfire-jenny-petty/

Research on the Prospective College Student Campus Visit and Its Impact on Matriculation. (2025). Retrieved from BHDP: https://www.bhdp.com/insights/research-prospective-college-student-campus-visit-and-its-impact-matriculation

Sinek, S. (2025). *Start with Why (15th Anniversary Edition): How Great Leaders Inspire Everyone to Take Action*. Penguin. Retrieved from https://simonsinek.com/books/start-with-why/

Steve Jobs. (2025, 26 September). Retrieved from Wikipedia: https://en.wikipedia.org/wiki/Steve_Jobs

Steve Wozniak. (2025, 26 September). Retrieved from Wikipedia: https://en.wikipedia.org/wiki/Steve_Wozniak

Strategic Plan. (2025). Retrieved from Ivy Tech Community College: https://www.ivytech.edu/about-ivy-tech/college-operations/strategic-plan/

Trust, but verify. (2025, 11 September). Retrieved from Wikipedia: https://en.wikipedia.org/wiki/Trust,_but_verify#:~:text=distrust%20and%20verify%22.-,Origins,a%20good%20basis%20for%20cooperation%22%20.

Tymoshchuk, O. (2021). *Font Readability Research: Key Difference Between Serif Vs Sans Serif Font.* Retrieved from Geniusee: https://geniusee.com/single-blog/font-readability-research-famous-designers-vs-scientists

Vaynerchuk, G. (2024). *Day Trading Attention: How to Actually Build Brand and Sales in the New Social Media World.* Harper Business.

Welding, L. (2025). *College Graduation Rates: Full Statistics.* Retrieved from Best Colleges: https://www.bestcolleges.com/research/college-graduation-rates/

Wells, P. C. (2024). *Clever Marketing Explained: Circus Analogy for Small Business Owners.* Retrieved from YouTube: https://www.youtube.com/watch?v=pxKIv6d2Xo4

ABOUT THE AUTHOR

BART CAYLOR'S PASSION FOR EDUCATION began at Anderson University, where he graduated Magna Cum Laude with much more than a degree. As a first-generation college student, Bart experienced firsthand how a Christian liberal arts education could alter the course of his life, and his career is a testament to those transformative years at AU.

Over the last 35 years, Bart has become a nationally recognized voice in higher education marketing, known for his practical, real-world approach and deep commitment to mission-driven institutions. His insights have been featured in the industry's top-ranked education blogs, and he's a sought-after speaker on topics ranging from marketing strategy and generative AI to the intersection of faith and education.

Before founding Caylor Solutions in 2011, Bart built a successful career working with global brands like AT&T, IAMs Pet Food, Motorola, RCA, and GE, as well as respected nonprofit organizations including the American Bible Society and the Lumina Foundation for Education. Today, he and his team serve colleges and universities of all sizes, combining best practices from the corporate, nonprofit, and education worlds to help institutions reach the right students with the right message.

Bart is also the bestselling author of *Chasing Mission Fit*, a guide for higher ed marketing leaders looking to clarify their institutional purpose and attract students who truly belong. He also co-hosts *The Higher Ed Marketer Podcast*, where he shares straightforward, actionable advice to help marketing and enrollment leaders face today's challenges with confidence. He has been named one of the "Top 10 Higher Ed Marketers You Should Follow" two years running by the Social Media Strategies Summit.

Bart continues to stay ahead of the curve for the future of marketing by consulting and delivering solutions in both print and digital mediums for his clients. When he needs to unplug, he spends time with his family and finds quiet moments to flyfish in the closest river.

ABOUT THE COMPANIES

CAYLOR SOLUTIONS

Your institution deserves to get noticed.

Caylor Solutions delivers [creative] solutions for education marketing. We craft [distinctive] brands and campaigns for [K–12 and higher ed] institutions—helping schools tell [authentic] stories that attract [mission-fit] students and drive [measurable] results through strategy, design, web, and [generative AI] innovation.

Founded in 2011, Caylor Solutions prides itself in providing customized branding, design and marketing solutions for colleges, universities, K-12 schools and educational organizations with one goal in mind: to advance education.

Through a diverse and experienced team of project managers, strategists, designers, writers and developers, Caylor Solutions strives to create impact for its clients through the development of strategic communication materials for a wide array of branding and marketing initiatives, such as:

- Mission-Fit Enrollment Marketing Solutions
- Enrollment Marketing Planning, Consulting, and Execution
- Comprehensive Communication Strategy & Development
- Fractional CMO Support & Strategic Leadership
- Brand Strategy, Identity, and Positioning
- Messaging Strategy, Development & Implementation
- Website Design, Development & Optimization
- Integrated Print & Digital Marketing Campaigns
- Audience & Persona Development
- GenAI Training and Executive Consulting

Visit caylor-solutions.com for a complete list of capabilities and case studies.

THE HIGHER ED MARKETER

With a heart for connection and impact, The Higher Ed Marketer was established to invite collaboration and foster a cycle of learning among higher ed marketers through content that both empowers marketers and builds community.

What was once a standalone podcast, The Higher Ed Marketer, has organically grown into a broad, knowledge-sharing entity for higher education and marketing professionals alike. Through various online resources, classes, books, the podcast and summits, The Higher Ed Marketer continues to highlight cutting-edge marketing tactics and inspire creative conversations.

Bart's love of learning and passion for innovative solutions have allowed him to dive head first into the world of Artificial Intelligence, particularly since the release of ChatGPT in late 2022. Through The Higher Ed Marketer, he leads the way in educating others and cultivating a community of learning in the ever evolving world of higher education marketing.

The Higher Ed Marketer remains committed to learning, unlearning and relearning in order to bring valuable content, resources and inspiring information to audience members for years to come. Find books, podcasts and more at thehigheredmarketer.com.